The Ducks Unlimited
GUIDE TO
SHOTGUNNING

Don Zutz

Ducks Unlimited, Inc.
Memphis, Tennessee

Text: Don Zutz
Executive Editor: Chuck Petrie
Editor: Art DeLaurier Jr.
Book Design: Monte Clair Finch

Published by Ducks Unlimited, Inc.
Julius Wall, President
Gene Henry, Chairman of the Board
Don Young, Executive Vice President

ISBN: 1-57223-393-1

Published May 2000

Ducks Unlimited, Inc.
The mission of Ducks Unlimited is to fulfill the annual life cycle needs of North American waterfowl by protecting, enhancing, restoring, and managing important wetlands and associated uplands. Since its founding in 1937, DU has raised more than $1.3 billion, which has contributed to the conservation of over 8.8 million acres of prime wildlife habitat in all fifty states, each of the Canadian provinces, and in key areas of Mexico. In the U.S. alone, DU has helped to conserve over 1.6 million acres of waterfowl habitat. Some 900 species of wildlife live and flourish on DU projects, including many threatened and endangered species.

Library of Congress Cataloging-in-publication Data
Zutz, Don
    The Ducks unlimited guide to shotgunning / Don Zutz.
      p.cm.
    A collection of the author's columns which appeared in Ducks unlimited magazine from 1990 to 1998
      ISBN 1-57223-393-1 (hardcover : alk. paper)
      1, Waterfowl shooting 2. Shotguns. I. Title: Guide to shotgunning. II. Title.

SK331 .Z86 2000
799.2'44--dc21

Dedicated to the
memory
of
Don Zutz,
shotgunning coach
for the ages

Table of Contents

Foreword..vii
Guns
  1. The Grand Old Guns of a Grand Old Era..............................3
  2. The Classic Pumps of Yesteryear 9
  3. The History and Handling of Waterfowling Doubles 13
  4. The Heavy Duck Gun...16
  5. Guns of a Feather 19
  6. The Evolution of Today's 10..23
  7. The 8-Gauge Lives 26
  8. Do American's Really Need British Doubles?......................28
  9. What's a Nice Gun Like You Doing in a Place Like This? 30

Loads and Ballistics
  10. Selecting Guns and Loads...37
  11. Guns and Loads for Hunting Over Decoys...........................42
  12. The 3½-inch 12-Gauge Magnum...47
  13. How Much from the 3-inch 20-Gauge? 49
  14. Full-Choke Steel..53
  15. Choking on Steel? Follow this Advice.................................57
  16. Beware of Choke-Tube Confusion 59
  17. Do We Still Have a Long-Range Duck Gun? 61

18. Steel Shot and the Side-by-Each 64
19. Shotshell Velocities 69
20. How Waterfowl Loads Changed with the Times 72
21. Moisture-Proofing Steel Loads 75
22. The Basics of Backboring 77

Shooting

23. Twenty Tips for Successful Wingshooting 85
24. Point-and-Shoot Shotguns 92
25. Stock Fit and Nonsense 96
26. The Eyes Have It 100
27. Peripheral Vision and Long Leads 103
28. The Trigger Hand's Role in Shotgunning 106
29. Learning to Score at Severe Angles 109
30. Hitting Long-Range Flushing Shots 114
31. High Birds 117
32. The Trouble with Sustained Lead Is... 120
33. How Nash Buckingham Did It 124
34. How Far Is It? Tips for Improving Your 127
    Range-Judging Skills
35. Exploding Skeet Shooting Myths 131
36. The Essence of Sporting Clays 134
37. The Makings of a Sporting Clays Gun 140
38. Barrel Length: The Long and the Short of It 144
39. Guns with a Second Chance 147

Tips and Tidbits

40. Taming Shotgun Recoil 153
41. On Really Cleaning a Shotgun 156
42. See Clearly Now 158
43. Clothes Make the Man 161
44. Have Shotgun, Will Travel, But... 165

Foreword

I first met Don Zutz in 1989 as part of a collection of writers assembled by gun and ammunition manufacturers to test the year's new product releases. As a relative newcomer to the profession, I did a lot of listening. Despite two days of lectures by the manufacturers' "experts," I came away learning considerably more about shotgunning from Don. Since that time, I frequently sought his opinion on a wide variety of shotgun and ballistic subjects, for his depth of knowledge on the topic was nothing short of encyclopedic.

Shortly after that first encounter, I joined the staff of *Ducks Unlimited* magazine where I began editing his column—which is to say that I merely read it. It was apparent from his text that Don had little interest in conjecture, for he was an analytical man who would meticulously test guns and loads to gauge their performance for himself. He seldom relied on data provided by manufacturers or others. Such devotion to accuracy was refreshingly rare in this business where anecdotal information is so frequently regurgitated as gospel.

It's hard to know how much Don influenced shotgunning in America, for in addition to being a bonafide shooting authority, he also was one of the most prolific writers of the genre. He served as shotgunning columnist for at least a half dozen national magazines and was always one of *Ducks Unlimited's* most popular authors.

He was a habitual shotgunner, frequently braving bitter January and February days in his home state of Wisconsin to pattern a gun or shoot a round of skeet. As a frequent practitioner, Don became one of the finest wingshots with whom I've ever hunted. And like most truly great shooters I've been around, he was forever humble about his own prowess. Readers gravitated to his column because he, like them, continually wanted to know how to be a better wingshot. Don did not have a penchant for pedigreed double guns; instead, he was a hunter who valued performance over style. His countless days slogging through wetlands and uplands gave him the practical knowledge to relate to waterfowlers and upland gunners everywhere. He encountered the same challenging shooting angles, gun malfunctions, and load failures that the rest of the shooting world faced, so he was prepared to address the concerns of the participating masses.

I sat in more than one duck blind where his columns ended great debates over such weighty issues as the virtues of sustained lead versus instinctive gunning, effective killing range, steel versus lead shot, the best long-range duck loads, autoloaders or pumps, etc. Few readers knew that Don also had a secondary career serving as an expert firearms witness in court trials all across the country. His no-nonsense demeanor and poker face served trial lawyers well, and his credentials were impeccable. It was that same credibility that helped foster his avid following among shotgunning readers.

For those who never met Don Zutz, the pages of this book represent a lifetime of lessons learned in the field and on the range. Read carefully and you'll benefit from one of the sport's greatest instructors. Becoming a better wingshot is a rewarding journey—the same path that Don forever helped so many others enjoy.

— Chris Dorsey —
Editor-in-Chief, Sports Afield

guns

66

The Browning Auto-5, made in Belgium,
became a favorite of American hunters.
– Don Zutz –

99

The Grand Old Guns
of a Grand Old Era

Whenever a younger man reached down to help him get out of the camouflaged boat, the bent and gimpy old fellow always used the same greeting. "This old shotgun of mine has taken more game than you'll ever see," he'd say. I respectfully believe he was wrong on that one; I've seen a lot of game, too. But he was my kind of guy, going with his boots on, hunting until his last sunset, and proud of his gun, which embodied his most precious possessions—memories.

The shotgun in question was a Winchester Model 1911 Self-Loader, and it typified the old hunter's heyday. For in his prime, shotgunning was going through a significant transition from doubles to repeaters and from black powder to smokeless. Some historians have dubbed the last 30 years of the nineteenth century the Golden Age of Shotgunning, because it was a time when shotguns improved while there was still an abundance of wild game.

But history has a momentum about it, and progress in gunmaking and shotshell technology continued into the early twentieth century despite dwindling game populations. Thus the grand old era of 1870-1930 was indeed filled with shotguns bearing grand old names. And, until the latter part of this period, these names were all stamped on doubles.

Perhaps the most ingenious of all Yankee gunmakers was Daniel M. "Uncle Dan" Lefever of Syracuse, New York, who beat everyone else by turning out America's first hammerless doubles in 1878. He followed this success with his Automatic Hammerless double, which had several take-up adjustments so that the owner could tighten the gun without gunsmithing services whenever wear occurred. There used to be an advertisement asking, "Have you ever seen a broken Lefever?" The answer was, "Not very often!" Lefever doubles have been underrated.

Although Colt has always been more famous for its revolvers, it also built hammer and hammerless doubles using foreign-made Damascus barrels. The hammer guns ran from 1878-1891; the hammerless models from 1883-1900. The hammerless guns were especially streamlined and nicely fitted and finished with expert hand checkering on English walnut. Competition caused Colt to drop its doubles at the turn of the century, but a critical inspection tells one that they were among the very best of the period.

By the 1880s, old hammer guns like this one were already becoming obsolete.

The now-treasured Parkers appeared in 1868 as Damascus-barreled hammer guns. Despite their current popularity among collectors, the Parkers were slow to improve. Hammerless Parkers didn't appear until 1889, and a close examination shows that they had a multitude of parts, whereas engineering theory holds to mechanical simplicity. But what Parker did, it did well, and the guns demonstrate good workmanship.

Add to that list the name of L. C. Smith doubles, which were made with a tapered rotary bolt that held them tight as a vault. Hammerless Smiths came on line in 1886 and lasted through World War II into the 1940s, the rotary bolt being a blessing when heavy loads of smokeless powders came along. Eventually, Ithaca and A. H. Fox also incorporated the rotary bolt device into their doubles.

The A. H. Fox Gun Company did not open until 1907, but it made some fine guns. For waterfowlers, the prized possession was the Model HE, also called the Super-Fox, which became available in the 1920s. Fox was looking to the future with this one—the venture being predicated on getting the utmost performance from the then-new 3-inch 12-gauge magnum shotshell and its $1^3/_8$-ounce charge. The Super-Fox generally had overbored barrels and choke constrictions regulated to throw tight patterns with coarse shot. Nash Buckingham's famous Burt Becker doubles were fashioned with Fox barreled actions.

Remington also built excellent hammerless doubles in the 1894 and 1990 models, and the higher grades are now treasured collector's items. Prior to that, the Remington-Whittmore was an appealing hammer double with classic lines.

The wave of the future broke in 1887, when Winchester brought out its 10- and 12-gauge lever-actioned shotguns, heralding the start of the repeating shotgun era. The lever actions, however, were mere stopgap items. They answered the demand for repeaters but, in reality, didn't provide the quick, smooth action a wingshot desires. The contemporary Burgess Gun, featuring a sliding pistol-grip mechanism, did not become a mechanical standard, nor did the Spencer and Roper pumps. They all rest now as noble ruins, although the Roper did mark the first use of screw-in choke tubes as early as the late 1860s and early 1870s.

5

The classic Browning Auto-5, the only successful autoloader from the first half of the twentieth century.

The breakthrough to successful repeaters came in 1893, when Winchester built its first hammer pumpgun. Built for black-powder pressures, the model 1893 was soon revamped for greater strength to handle the pressure of smokeless powder and renamed the Model 1897, alias the Model 97. It went on to become a favorite with upland hunters as well as waterfowlers. Not possessed of a truly slick pumping stroke, the Model 97 did have a trim profile and was a natural pointer, with gripping points that brought the shooter's hands quite close to the bore's axis for optimal use of natural hand-eye coordination.

When Remington brought out its first pumpgun in 1907, the company chose a hammerless, but continued the Winchester Model 97's concern for pointability. Remington did this, according to an old catalog, by ensuring "the grip of the stock being more nearly in line with the barrel than any other design of repeating shotgun yet produced." These Remingtons, which are better known as the Models 10 and 29, also emphasize hand-to-bore relationship for fine pointing qualities.

Winchester's Model 12 entered the scene in 1912, and in its early stages had a grip and spool-like forend akin to those of the Model 97. Winchester advertising called it "the perfect repeater," and not many people argued. The Model 12 became a prestigious piece, and even today it commands a premium price among collectors and traders.

Autoloading shotguns entered the scene at the very turn of the century, when John M. Browning's Auto-5 became available. Everyone knew that a shotshell's recoil energy and/or powder gases could operate an autoloading action, but gun tinkerers couldn't get them to work dependably with the plethora of loads on the market—black powder, semi-smokeless and smokeless—until Browning came along with his long-recoil system and its adjustable friction devices and shock absorbers. The Browning Auto-5 not only became the favorite of hunters, but it also remained the sole successful autoloading shotgun design of the first half of the twentieth century.

The Browning Auto-5 was made in Belgium, but Remington and then Savage were licensed to build the gun stateside. Savage's was the Model 720. Remington's version was the 5-shot Model 11, which was introduced in 1911 and had a tremendous following among duck hunters, remaining in production until 1948. Remington would later add a three-shot Model 11 Sportsman with a bulkier forearm to comply with the then-new federal three-shot limit for waterfowling. Although heavy, the Model 11 pointed well, swung smoothly, and became a favorite of early skeet shooters. When heavy, high-velocity shotshells came along as progressive-burning powders were improved, Remington followed the Fox Gun Company's lead in making some overbored barrels for the Model 11 (and also the Model 31 pumpgun) to handle these charges more efficiently.

And what about the old fellow's Winchester Model 1911? The Self-Loader is an interesting relic. Winchester never did come to terms with Browning and subsequently came up with its own Model 1911 design. This was, however, the long-recoil system without all the vital Browning-patented features such as the operating handle and friction and shock-absorbing devices. The Winchester thus became known as a stock splitter because of its hammering recoil, and its lack of an operating handle made it awkward to load and unload. Consequently, its sales trailed the Browning and Remington autoloaders significantly.

This was too bad, because the mechanically ill-fated Winchester Model 1911 actually had a modern feel to it, having more rounded lines than the Browning Auto-5 with its humpbacked receiver, and it pointed nicely. But like so many of the fowling pieces mentioned here, the Winchester Model 1911 Self-Loader is treasured mainly as a golden memory of a better day, and a better time. Just ask any old gimpy veteran of the marshland.

The Classic Pumps of Yesteryear

In the first half of the twentieth century, Captain Charles Askins Sr. was America's shotgun guru. Writing in his 1910 tome, *The American Shotgun*, Askins opined that "the pump repeater is merely a halfway house on the march to an automatic." Simply stated, he believed the pump was not long for this world, and that hunters would switch to the semi-automatic as soon as it was perfected. To Askins, then, the pumpgun was a stopgap design, a steppingstone to better things.

It didn't work out that way, of course. Instead of giving way to the newfangled semi-autos, pumpguns retained a loyal following to remain a potent factor in American shotgun manufacturing. Out of this came some classics in concept and construction.

Although not the slickest pump, Winchester's early Model 1897 hammer pump had superb pointing qualities. Its overall low profile gave hand-to-bore and hands-in-line relationships closely akin to those of side-by-sides of that era. Amazingly, this Model 97 hammer pump lasted in Winchester's line from 1897 to 1957, despite the fact that, beginning in 1912, Winchester had launched another classically built pump, the trim and compact Model 12.

There is little doubt that the Model 12 was one of the best pumps ever made, and it quickly became a winner in skeet and trap. In 1935, the Model 12 Heavy Duck Gun was announced with 3-inch chambers, the first-ever 12-gauge magnum repeater. But the 1930s

©BILL BUCKLEY

A modern classic? The Remington Model 870 is an old favorite among waterfowlers.

were the age of the Depression, and many hunters weren't yet magnum minded. Hence, it isn't surprising that the Model 12 Heavy Duck Gun sold below expectations.

Shortly after its introduction, the Model 12 Heavy Duck Gun was given a shorter stock (13⅝ inches) and a lead slug in the butt to offset barrel weight and recoil. High quality eventually did in the Model 12, however. All of its parts were machined—not made of castings or stampings—and carefully fitted, which made it expensive to produce.

Always competitive, Remington also produced some classic pumps prior to World War II. In keeping with a concern for pointing qualities, Remington's introduction of the Model 1908 hammerless slide-action proudly stated, "It handles fast and balances perfectly, due in large measure to the grip of stock being more nearly in line with the barrel than any other design of repeating shotgun yet produced." When the Remington Models 10 and 29 pumpguns followed, they also had the same features.

But the early Remington pumps were bottom ejectors (like today's Ithaca Model 37 and Browning BPS) and didn't appeal to skeet and trap shooters the way the side-ejecting Winchester Model 12 did. In 1931, then, Remington brought out a fast-stroking pump

Winchester Model 12

known simply as the Model 31. It became known for its distinctive ball-bearing action. Made of machined parts, the Model 31 Remington was, along with the Model 12, one of the highest-quality pumps of the prewar era. The Model 31 Remington was never made in a 3-inch magnum grade. But when high-velocity 1¼-ounce duck loads came along, Remington did make some overbored waterfowl barrels for it. Such barrels are hard to find today.

There was one final classic to come out of the 1930s, Ithaca's Model 37. When Remington dropped the bottom-ejecting models,

Lou Smith of Ithaca picked it up and, by 1937, brought to market his version of the concept. Ithaca's Model 37 was lighter than Remington Models 1908, 1910, and 1927 had been. Still solidly machined of steel parts and smooth of stroke, the Model 37 appealed to lots of hunters. In addition, the prewar deluxe and target grades had gorgeous American black walnut.

After World War II, inflation increased the cost of shotgun production, and it soon became obvious to manufacturers that they had to change models and manufacturing techniques, because the public wouldn't pay as much for a pump as it would for a double or semi-auto. Remington's Model 31 was discontinued in 1950; Winchester's "perfect repeater," the Model 12, was dropped in 1964.

Nevertheless, one firm—Ithaca—continues to manufacture a well-made pump. After several financial failings, different ownerships, and wheel spinning, Ithaca is once again producing the Model 37s it did in the days of yesteryear. It will be interesting to see how this born-again classic fares as we enter the twenty-first century.

This hunter is shooting one the the best pumps ever made—a Winchester Model 12.

The History and Handling
of Waterfowling Doubles

Delightfully fast and lightweight side-by-sides have always been associated with upland gunning. The British game gun—a 12-gauge double, typically weighing 6¼ to 6½ pounds—set the standard for this type. Game guns are built so that their halfweight rests squarely between a shooter's hands, while the remaining heft is balanced evenly between the muzzles and the butt. This provides for quick, smooth pivoting, which is essential while shooting swift-flushing and driven birds on the moors and swales of Great Britain.

Traditional game guns have a straight grip, splinter forend, and, most frequently, twin triggers. Their profile is indeed racy, which has made them popular among many American sportsmen. If these famous side-by-sides have a weakness, however, it is recoil. Because of their light overall weight, game guns can kick excessively. To offset heavy recoil, the Brits historically opted for light loads—typically 1½-inch cartridges with an ounce of lead shot.

As the British learned long ago, the lightweight game gun is hardly ideal for waterfowling. While light loads were the rule for shooting upland birds, the hunters of the United Kingdom didn't hesitate to pound heavy loads downrange when waterfowling conditions demanded it. The 8-gauge was once rather common in Britain, and they homeloaded extra-long shotshells long before magnum mania swept the U.S.

chapter three

With the advent of smokeless powders, gunsmiths began building heavier doubles with more robust frames. Barrel walls were thickened to counter increased gas pressure. As a result, 12-gauge doubles reached weights of eight to nine pounds, and 10-gauge magnums tipped the scales at 11 pounds or more.

The heavyweight, magnum-chambered double caught on in the U.S. between the world wars, especially in the 1930s, when progressive-burning, smokeless powders made the use of heavier shot charges possible. Ithaca produced some of the initial 10-gauge magnums for 3½-inch loads; L. C. Smith built 12-gauges chambered for 3-inch magnum hulls for waterfowling; and A. H. Fox offered its Super-Fox, or HE Grade, 12-gauge doubles chambered for 3-inch magnums and slightly overbored to achieve greater pattern density. Later, Winchester modified its Model 21 side-by-side into a Heavy Duck Gun chambered for 3-inch shells.

In catalog listings, these doubles became known as wildfowl or waterfowl models. They typically were built with semi- or full-pistol grips for better lifting purchase and recoil control. Twin triggers remained standard among overseas brands, while American gunsmiths preferred single triggers.

The handling dynamics of a bona fide waterfowling double are noticeably different than those of the lightweight game gun. The heavily walled barrels of waterfowling doubles create a weight-forward condition that, along with the overall weight, slows the mounting process and initial swing speed. As a result, many hunters find the heftier wildfowl doubles simply to be too much gun. For those with the strength to handle these heavy fowling pieces, however, the weight isn't a drawback. Once a shooter gets the heavy barrels moving, momentum is easily sustained for a smooth swing and positive follow-through.

In addition to their prodigious weight, the specialized waterfowling doubles also lost favor because misguided individuals claimed that it is too difficult to point their broad muzzles accurately. Such criticism, however, is not based on fact and is only made by those with serious flaws in their shooting technique.

The popularity of waterfowl doubles has also been diminished by the popularity of over-unders and repeaters, as well as the mandated use of steel shot, which will ruin the barrels of many classic heavy doubles. While several new steel-shot-compatible models have been developed in recent years, they have had only limited commercial success. Waterfowling doubles have become rare artifacts in North America—which is a pity, because few guns have more artistry in them than the classic side-by-sides.

chapter four

The Heavy Duck Gun

Magnum-chambered repeating guns are pretty much taken for granted by waterfowlers these days. Practically every 12- and 20-gauge pumpgun is chambered for the 3-inch hull. Certain slide-actions stretch that to $3\frac{1}{2}$ inches for the 10-gauge magnum or the $3\frac{1}{2}$-inch 12-gauge. Indeed, such repeaters are as common as a Pepsi machine outside a mini-mart.

But it wasn't always so. Until the mid-1930s, lengthy magnum chambers were used solely in break-action guns. Ithaca made the first $3\frac{1}{2}$-inch magnum 10 doubles; the Fox Gun Company of Philadelphia turned out some specialized 3-inch 12s. But gunmakers weren't thrilled with the expense of redesigning and retooling for magnum-grade repeaters.

It wasn't until 1935 that the first legitimate magnum-grade repeater was announced, and it was 1936 before most dealers could get them. This was the Winchester Model 12 variant known as the Heavy Duck Gun. For nearly a double decade it was destined to be the only magnum-chambered repeater made stateside.

In general, the Heavy Duck Gun can be described as a Model 12 beefed up to handle the stresses of magnum loads. At first, some were skeptical of the Heavy Duck Gun's weight. Early catalog listings had it at $8\frac{1}{2}$ pounds, but that was soon changed to 8 pounds and 11 ounces for the 30-inch-barreled model. Those versions with 32-inch barrels and raised, matted ribs added a few more ounces. Despite the extra forward weight, I have always found the 30-inch Heavy Duck Guns to be relatively easy handling. The slightly heavier barrel is offset nicely by a lead slug in the butt.

Despite our current magnum mania, the Model 12 Heavy Duck Gun was the only repeater in the magnum mode until Remington's Model 870 was given a 3-inch chamber in 1955. Actually, the market wasn't receptive of the magnum concept until the late 1950s and the soaring '60s. Hunters apparently thought they had enough power in the then-new $1/4$-ounce high-velocity load for the standard 12, a high-brass offering that had a published velocity around 1,330 feet per second. Of the 2 million or so Model 12s ever made, only a small percentage were Heavy Duck Guns. In his authoritative book *The Winchester Model Twelve*, former Winchester engraver George Madis notes that extant records indicate a sale of only 18,800 Heavy Duck

©BILL BUCKLEY

Chances are only 1 in 100 that this hunter's Model 12 is a Heavy Duck Gun.

Guns. But some Winchester records were lost or destroyed early in World War II to fudge that final figure, and there were undoubtedly more produced. Exactly how many more is a good question.

Although Winchester catalogs carried specs and prices only for plain versions of the Heavy Duck Gun, some extremely limited runs were made with ventilated ribs and skeet-grade (or Super Field) wood, meaning a beavertail forearm that's checkered, not grooved, along with an advanced grade of walnut with grip checkering. Another rarity is a Heavy Duck Gun with a straight grip, which was also available as an option but seldom ordered. These are truly valuable Heavy Duck Guns, and they do not come cheaply among knowledgeable traders and collectors.

The Winchester Model 12 Heavy Duck Gun was dropped in 1963, about the same time Winchester discontinued all guns that were still being carefully assembled of machined parts.

Has steel shot made a noble ruin of the Model 12 Heavy Duck Gun? I doubt it. The hunter who owns one or who is twinged by nostalgia to buy one can still use it. I spent part of a duck season with one recently and my micrometer couldn't find any changes in barrel dimensions. The gun's barrel walls seem thick enough to handle the stresses of steel shot passage. About the only modification I'd consider were I to use one continually is having the choke opened mildly to eliminate the potential for ring bulging. Dropping back to improved-modified choke, something around a .28 to .30 inch of constriction, might do the job without disrupting patterns.

The first magnum repeater is still a viable fowling piece. When Winchester developed it, the company's officials decided against listing it in deluxe and pigeon grades because they thought it would become a workhorse of a gun that would see rough usage and nasty weather. In that they were right. But the gun has withstood the test of time, too. And for that it shouldn't be considered just the first of its breed, but a classic among pumpguns.

Guns of a Feather

Upland bird hunters who really get into their sport seem to eventually gravitate to the smaller gauges or lightweight 12s, and that's just fine. A sleek 28-gauge double or a trim 20-gauge autoloader is a fine fit for a grouse covert or bobwhite hunt.

But the smaller and lighter shotguns have a different dynamic than heftier models. Lacking weight, and generally being short of barrel (so many of these guns have barrels of just 21 to 25 inches these days), they contribute little to swing smoothness, momentum, and follow-through. While they are easy to carry and virtually spring into action on a surprise flush, there's more to shotgunning than carrying ease and explosive starts. A gun with such qualities is often regarded as "whippy," as it'll start faster than the hunter can control it and then die from lack of momentum.

The same isn't true for heavier guns or those with longer barrels. They'll start a little slower, accelerate to and through the target, and retain smoothness and energy into a definite follow-through. Some of the heavier guns are said to "swing themselves" once they're started. But 30-inch-barreled heavyweights aren't popular in the uplands these days, so how can we get optimal results with the lesser bores and lightweights?

©CHRIS DORSEY

Dynamic upland guns like this one require equally dynamic handling and timing.

A COMPLETE PIVOT

There are times when heavy, long-barreled shotguns will cover up a human error by supplying the continued swing energy needed for a lead and then a follow-through. The hunter may have stopped or slowed his movement, but the gun keeps going. Without the forward momentum inherent in a longer-barreled gun, however, an uplander must supply the continued pivot himself. This can be done by footwork or by a conscious rotation from the waist. In either case, it must be done. Without that physical pivot, an upland hunter may throw a lot of patterns well behind birds due to failure to follow through with a short, light gun. Some off-season practice on hand-thrown clays or skeet can help ingrain that pivot.

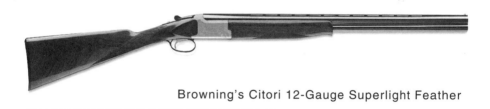

Browning's Citori 12-Gauge Superlight Feather

REDUCED HAND ACTION

Another problem in using lightweights is hand action. Aggressive hand and arm action can yank that type of upland delicacy off target and throw the entire mount, point, swing, and follow-through sequence out of kilter. This kind of gun handling isn't smooth or coordinated, of course. It's wild and crazy, and many such guns are easily poked too far ahead of the bird too soon.

How does one overcome this potential for overlapping a light, short upland bird gun? Mainly by minimizing the aggressiveness of both hands and arms. Employ a very tender grip so that you don't jerk the gun ahead of the target. Let the piece merely lie in your hands like soft-shell eggs. Excessive hand action perhaps can't jerk an $8^{1}/_{2}$-pound 12-gauge off line, but it sure can overpower a $5^{1}/_{2}$-pound 20-gauge double!

Timing is also a critical factor when wingshooting with lightweight upland guns. Since the gun starts quickly and flashes through the target rapidly, the trigger pull must jibe with the gun's speed. The hunter who whips up his slim, trim 20-bore and then delays the trigger pull will either shoot well ahead or behind the mark.

With a lightweight bird gun, then, the move-mount-shoot sequence is a shorter, more compact action than it is with long, heavy shotguns that unlimber more slowly. If any one rule can be laid down regarding the dynamic bird guns, it is this: Don't try to track and measure off a precise forward allowance. Short-barreled, lightweight smallbore bird guns are at their worst when handled deliberately. Dynamic upland guns demand equally dynamic handling and timing.

The Evolution of Today's 10

During the late nineteenth century, 10-gauge shotguns were more popular among clay-target shooters and hunters than 12-gauges. However, these weren't the same 10-gauges we know today. Many had Damascus barrels chambered for 2¹/₂-inch shotshells loaded with just 1¹/₄ ounces of shot. Those 10-bore doubles of yesteryear were also lighter by several pounds, because they didn't need thick, heavy barrels to withstand high bore pressures, nor did they require beefy internal parts to withstand firing stresses.

I have owned a couple of 10-gauge doubles from the past, and they had better handling qualities than any modern 10. I can understand how early-day sportsmen could take 10s afield and wield them efficiently. The same goes for clay-target and live-pigeon shooters.

The modern sportsman knows an entirely different 10-gauge. Whereas it was once a highly versatile weapon during the late 1880s, the 10 has become a rather specialized gauge today, featuring the heaviest legal loads and massive guns to withstand them. The transition began during the 1920s, when improvements in progressive-burning powders came along. Initially, the 10-gauge was given a longer, 2⁷/₈-inch hull and a 1⁵/₈-ounce shot charge, fired at 1,275 feet per second by a powder charge equivalent to 4¹/₂ to 4³/₄ drams of black powder.

chapter six

Some gun writers of the period, like theoretical scientists, looked further ahead. The spacious .775-inch bore of the 10 could accommodate more powder and shot. A trio of men heavily promoted the concept of a bigger 10: John M. Olin, a dedicated hunter who was also head of the giant Olin Chemical Corporation (which owned Winchester); Captain Charles Askins, who was arguably America's best shotgun writer at the time and was the arms and ammunition editor for *Outdoor Life*; and Elmer Keith, who was not yet a household name but was becoming established as a writer who liked big holes in his rifle, pistol, and shotgun muzzles. Olin ramrodded the development of a modern 10 through Winchester-Western arms and ammo, Askins promoted it in his monthly columns, and Keith carried the torch for the big 10 in later years.

The result was the 3$\frac{1}{2}$-inch shotshell, stuffed with 2 ounces of

Browning BPS 10-Gauge Hunter

lead shot with a published velocity of 1,210 fps. The charge of progressive-burning, smokeless powder was equivalent to about 4$\frac{1}{2}$ drams of black powder. Ithaca agreed to make some side-by-sides for this whopping magnum shell. Eventually, the company made 1,000 of them. They are now collectibles of considerable value.

Because the slow-burning powders of magnum shells exerted high bore pressures, gun makers built 10-gauges with thick barrels, which dramatically increased gun weights to 10$\frac{1}{2}$ to 11$\frac{1}{2}$ pounds. Understandably, hunters were less than enthusiastic about handling such iron monsters. As a result, instead of the 10-gauge becoming more popular among shooters, it actually lost favor.

Another reason why the 10 lost ground was the development of 3-inch magnum 12-gauge ammunition, which was loaded with progressively heavier shot charges of up to 1$\frac{7}{8}$ ounces. Why would anyone want to shoulder an 11-pound 10-gauge when an 8$^{1}/_{2}$-pound 12-gauge could throw an almost equivalent shot charge?

The mighty 10 was relegated to obscurity until goose populations began to rebound during the late 1960s and 1970s. The gradual transition to steel also helped the 10-gauge magnum. Since steel shot of any given size is about one-third lighter than lead, it is quickly slowed by air resistance (drag), providing lower velocity and energy, especially at long ranges. Hence, heavy steel shot, such as BBBs and Ts, was needed to deliver the energy and, consequently, killing power of lead 2s and BBs. The 10 filled this niche perfectly, as its huge hulls held the heaviest shot charges of large steel shot.

Thus the age of steel brought back the 10-gauge to serve a practical purpose, perhaps vindicating the early pioneers of these prodigious arms.

chapter seven

The 8-Gauge Lives

The gun caught my eye as I spent a weekend perusing the magnificent firearms displays at the Buffalo Bill Historical Center in Cody, Wyoming. It was a 4-gauge, single-shot percussion gun that was made specially for Thomas G. Bennett, the son-in-law of Oliver F. Winchester, and it brought to mind the era of big boomers and a current mild interest in the 8-gauge.

The waterfowling guns of the latter half of the nineteenth century were commonly made in 4- or 8-gauge. The 8-gauges were doubles; the 4s were single shots. The 4-gauge was typically a single shot instead of a double barrel because it was easier for gunners to handle the lighter, one-barreled version. And they were popular then because, like the 10-gauge today, they could deliver heavy shot charges within safe chamber pressure limits. A shotgun's bore also acts like a safety valve: the larger it is, the quicker it bleeds off the potentially destructive pressures of gas expansion.

The 8-gauge has a typical bore diameter of .835 inch compared to .775 inch for the 10-gauge and .729 inch for the 12. Cases for it seem to have run from 3 inches to 3¼ inches, and the old waterfowling loads carried about 7 grams of black powder under 2 ounces of lead shot. However, books from the era list everything from 1¾- to 2½-ounce shot charges.

Read British sporting literature and you'll find that these big boomers were often used to flock shoot, after which the hunters picked up lesser 12-gauges to wade into the salt and collect the cripples. It is hardly a sporting concept today, but that was then and this is now. And surprisingly enough, there is still some interest in the 8-gauge, which obviously is illegal for modern waterfowling.

Guys simply like to shoot the old boomers. So much so, in fact, that Ballistic Products Inc. (20015 75th Avenue, North, Corcoran, Minnesota 55340-9456) has brought out a one-piece plastic shot cup wad for it and also stocks the traditional card/filler wad columns. New 8-gauge plastic hulls are available too.

Who needs an 8-gauge? Nobody, perhaps. But this does keep collectors and nostalgia buffs in business. Reloading data? Ask BPI.

Meanwhile, the 8-gauge lives—as a shootable collectible.

Do American Hunters
Really Need British Doubles?

The traditional British double is known as a "game gun." It sports a straight grip, splinter forend, and is trim and elegant. Game guns are also dynamic. Handmade, the 12-gauges weigh between 6¼ and 6¾ pounds with 28- to 30-inch barrels, and their weight is concentrated between the shooter's hands so that these guns respond and pivot effortlessly. They are joys to point and swing.

But game guns are also expensive. Used ones run from about $5,000 in well-worn condition to $25,000 or more. Order a new one, and the price could be $35,000 to $50,000 with a three-year wait for the finished gun.

Few hunters can afford to pay that much for a bird gun, of course. In recent seasons, however, many American sportsmen have opted for less expensive copies of British doubles. They don't get the same delightful weight-balance features, but for some reason they feel that this racy configuration is magic afield.

Do American hunters really need British game guns or their copies? Are over-unders and repeaters so terribly inferior to straight-gripped side-by-sides? Let the British answer: When it comes to sporting clays, a game that emulates field-style gunning, virtually every Englishman will opt for an over-under or a gas-operated autoloader. Why? Experience has proved that stack barrels and semi-autos simply

Though sleek and elegant, doubles such as this Winchester 12-gauge, modeled after the classic British sidelock, may not outperform your favorite repeater.

score better. I've been to several world and Pan-American sporting clays events, and the side-by-sides have been conspicuous in their absence. Indeed, the Brits still use the side-by-side for some sporting clays, but when they do it's a special competition limited to only horizontal doubles so that everyone is equal.

Also, remember that the British game gun was mainly developed for high-angle fire on driven game, whereas much American uplanding is done on low-flying flushing game. There is a difference. High targets can be seen atop the bores, while low-flying birds can be blotted out by the broad barrels of a traditional double. Thus the narrower pointing plane of an over-under or autoloader provides better all-around target visibility.

This doesn't mean the side-by-side is totally dead. It'll still bag game. But we've reached a point where nostalgia plays a role rather than optimal efficiency. The next person to win the world sporting clays championship will have an over-under or gas-operated autoloader in his hands, not a British game gun. What we do need, however, are gunmakers who pay as much attention to the weight distribution on over-unders and autoloaders as the Brits did on their classic doubles.

What's a Nice Gun Like You Doing in a Place Like This?

Whenever I got a new baseball as a kid, my mother would lay down the law. "Now, don't get it all scuffed up!"

But what's a baseball for? So I'd sneak it out behind the shed where we'd whack it around until it was grass-stained and lopsided. That beat just looking at it.

And the same is true for shotguns. If perfectly white baseballs were made for hitting, finely fitted and finished shotguns were made for hunting and shooting. Shotgun buffs can't get hung up by the "don't scratch it" syndrome. The attributes of a high-grade shotgun—balance, fit, feel, trimness of line, fancy walnut, elegant décor, and an overall attention to detail—provide enhanced pointing and swinging dynamics along with pride of ownership.

Before steel shot came along, I sloshed around duck country with a fine European-made over-under that is now worth about $3,000. It was smooth swinging on high mallards while still responsive enough for woodies twisting through tree crowns. One day while slogging through knee-deep muck as I jump-shot an alder-rimmed slough, I met a gun-savvy hunter who looked admiringly at the over-under and, shaking his head sadly, asked, "What's a nice gun like that doing in a place like this?"

Nice guns, like this Beretta 686, have a lot more going for them than good looks.

"Performing," I replied, "and adding a bit of its own beauty to the day." I guess you've got to be a dedicated gun nut to understand that reply, but it's the same reasoning that's applied by sports car enthusiasts who treasure the Ferrari, Porsche, and Corvette over a family sedan. They perform and have eye appeal.

It has always been interesting for me to note the double standard many sportsmen apply in their equipment selection. They will spend $30,000 to $50,000 for a four-wheel-drive recreational vehicle that they slam through the woods, spin through mud, hammer into deep snow, and let stand outside in any and all sorts of rain and sleet. The tremendous cost and depreciation of such a vehicle doesn't faze them. Yet I've known the same people to protest the prices of guns that range but a couple hundred dollars beyond those advertised by discount stores.

For anyone who loves the aesthetics of a hunt, then, each dollar spent on a fine gun outlasts the pleasures of those spent on an RV. Life just seems a little better with a fine gun in the blind—whether it's scratched or not.

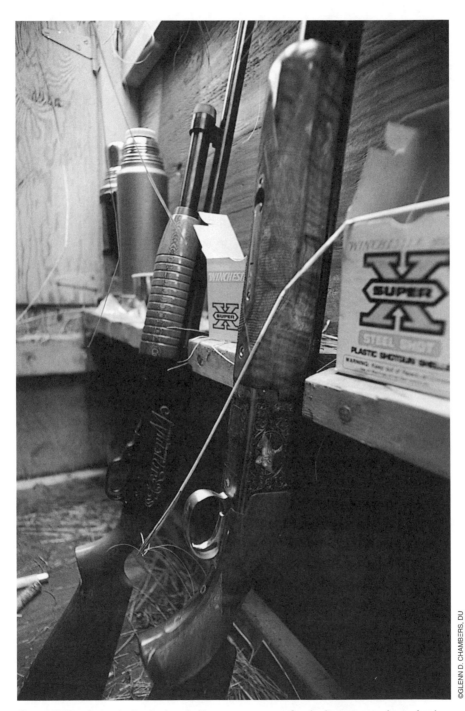

Sometimes beauty is, indeed, its own excuse for being—even in a duck blind.

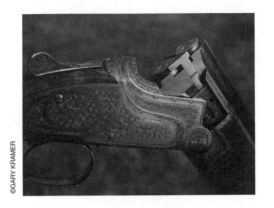

©GARY KRAMER

loads and ballistics

Selecting Guns and Loads

When lead shot was legal, the subject of gun and load selections for waterfowling was a long and involved treatise. In those days, a hunter might consider everything from a 28-gauge and No. 1^1/2s for decoying birds to the 10-gauge magnum and No. 4 buckshot for geese. That covers a lot of guns and ballistics.

But steel shot has simplified things. Because steel shot is lighter than lead shot of any given diameter, we now concentrate on heavier shot sizes such as No. 1s, BBs, BBBs, and 1's. To get enough of these bulky pellets into the pattern, we find that 10- and 12-gauge guns are the most legitimate choices. The lesser gauge loads not only don't pack much shot overall (the 16-gauge, for example, doesn't even hold a full ounce), but they aren't offered with steel sizes larger than the No. 2, which is a marginal pellet on geese. Neither the 16-gauge nor the 20-gauge can hold an ounce of steel 1s or BBs because of the wasted air space between those larger pellets; consequently, their clean-killing ranges are limited.

The best guns for optimal efficiency with the larger steel pellets are the 3-inch 12-gauge magnum, the 3^1/2-inch 12-gauge magnum, and the born-again 10-gauge magnum. Each has its strong points, each has its weaknesses.

©CHRIS DORSEY

Decisions, decisions. Though steel shot has simplified things, choosing
the right gun and load still merits some consideration.

The 3-inch 12 is quite effective with 1¼-ounce loads of steel 1s, BBs, and BBBs. However, the 1¼-ounce charge begins to run short on pellet density when it comes to T-shot and F-shot, and crippling can occur due to holes in the pattern at longer distances. For shooting inside 50 yards, though, the 3-inch 12 holds its own, and most such guns have weight and dimensions that typical hunters can handle with relative ease.

On the opposite extreme is the 3½-inch 10-gauge magnum, which can throw a full 1¾-ounce charge of steel shot to sweeten patterns at long range. But 10-gauge magnums, alas, are heavy pieces with bulkier dimensions, and many casual hunters find they simply can't handle them. You must be very honest about these things when it comes to good wingshooting. More gun isn't always better if you can't generate a smooth, crisp swing with it.

That's where the 3½-inch 12-gauge magnum comes in. The idea behind the Roman candle 12 is to give the hunter a lighter, trimmer gun, but one that delivers a load of 10-gauge proportions. The basic 3½-inch 12-gauge shotshell has a 1⁹⁄₁₆-ounce charge of steel shot, and it patterns quite well with the big Ts and Fs. Guns chambered for the 3½-inch 12 will also shoot 2¾- and 3-inch 12-gauge loads, so there is some versatility here.

Regardless of which gauge and chamber length a waterfowler prefers, he can get it in practically any action type. All are made in over-under, pump, side-by-side, and autoloading persuasions of one brand or another. Which is best? It's pretty much a personal matter. Pumpguns have always proved reliable and are generally the least expensive. However, it must be noted that youngsters and other beginners are often befuddled by the pumping stroke. Autoloaders generate less noticeable recoil with heavy loads, and over-unders can be very natural pointers. Whatever fits a hunter physically and financially can generally be justified.

Which barrel length? The trend is toward barrels shorter than the once traditional 30- and 32-inchers. With today's modern powders, a 28-inch barrel combines adequate ballistics with good handling. It is a legitimate length for all-around waterfowling regardless of gauge, although some hunters carry it a step further and do better with a 26-

chapter ten

Over-under, side-by-side, pump, or autoloader? The choice is usually
a matter of personal preference.

inch barrel on their magnum 10s. The point is, the old Long Tom era has run its course.

When it comes to load selection, steel has rewritten the rules of the game. For decoying ducks, No. 3s are about the smallest steel pellets that I'd recommend for positive performance. Steel 4s, which were widely used in the early days of non-toxic shot, proved unworthy of the hunter's trust and may have been one reason why steel shot was criticized as a crippler. Steel No. 2s have a following for ducks, and they are good over decoys. But for passing birds of varying distances, steel 1s or BBs are far better choices.

For jump-shooting, heavy pellets are needed to give deep penetration on angling and outgoing birds. Here again, steel No. 1s and BBs are tops. Some hunters think 1s and BBs too potent for ducks, but field experience tells me differently. Although geese can be taken cleanly to 45 yards with steel 1s, steel BBs are a better choice even at moderate distances for their added energies. As a solid all-around goose load, the triple-B (BBB) is excellent, splitting the difference between the energy of T-shot and the pattern density of BBs. Despite its vaunted per-pellet energy, the big F-shot has been criticized by serious hunters for its patterning weakness at long range, which can cause crippling, one-pellet hits.

Choke selection for steel-shot loads is a book-length subject. Do not be deceived into believing that open chokes (skeet and improved-cylinder) are ideal. For practical purposes, a solid modified choke or improved-modified is a better choice as an all-around constriction for waterfowling. When hardened full-choked tubes are supplied, they will indeed deliver tight patterns despite popular (and misleading) mythology to the contrary. The best answer is to devote a Saturday afternoon to test patterning. Then go out to the skeet field or sporting clays course and become totally familiar with your equipment.

Guns and Loads for Hunting Over Decoys

B efore the use of live decoys was outlawed, waterfowlers could often count on their pen-raised birds attracting wild ducks and geese to within relatively close shooting range. Many wildfowl were fooled by the siren song of live decoys tethered in front of blinds, and fell victim to well-hidden gunners. Improved calling techniques and mass-produced plastic decoys are used to attract waterfowl these days. And there's no doubt these are extremely effective elements when used properly.

The mere mention of hunting waterfowl over decoys often tends to make one conjure up visions of close-range shooting, as well as thoughts of open-choked guns and lighter loads of fine shot. But there's more to it than that; the subject is not without its complexities. The advent of steel shot, spooky birds, and itchy trigger fingers prompt some serious, in-depth thinking about this approach to the sport of waterfowling.

The question at the heart of this subject is: Are you really going to wait until the birds are in easy range, cupping their wings and settling in, or are you going to lose your sense of discipline and s-t-r-e-t-c-h your barrel when skittish flights make only one high pass or merely skirt the very outer fringe of your spread? This is an important point, because an extra 10 to 20 yards can turn an effective close-range outfit into a crippler. You'll see this for yourself when you shoot an improved-cylinder pattern at 20 to 25 yards and then run a second pattern at 35 yards. Besides that, the energy of the lighter steel pellets drops off sharply as the distance increases.

Assuming that a hunter does have the self-control to wait until birds show up over his decoys, an improved-cylinder choke can work effectively. And if the shooting takes place in tight quarters, such as a flooded timber tract where woodies and mallards funnel below the tree crowns, even a skeet gun can suffice. Don't be misled by the popular myth that open-choked guns invariably give riflelike patterns with steel loads. They don't! An open-choked shotgun may deliver patterns of the full-choke variety with the bigger steel BBs, Ts and Fs, but with finer pellets these open chokes will normally spread them about more liberally.

Which pellet sizes are we talking about for ducks and geese over decoys? When shooting is quite close, such as in the flooded oaks, No. 5s do nicely. In general, steel 5s have about the energy of lead No. 7s, and that'll do for 20- to 25-yard chances. When I first used steel 5s on drake woodies in a timbered drainage ditch area, I found that I liked them better than steel 4s. Why? Apparently the steel 5s put more pellets on target than the steel 4s. And with the range being close enough for the 5s to retain adequate energy, the multiple-hit performances anchored more birds cleanly. However, there is a definite range limitation with steel 5s, which is where the self-discipline part comes in.

There are steel No. 6s on the market, but my experience with them has not been exciting. These pellets have the energy level of lead No. 8s, which were hardly ever bona fide waterfowling pellets, and they have an obvious lack of impact on birds as heavily covered by down as mallards. The difference between steel 5s and 6s may seem scant on a

©GARY R. ZAHM

Birds that hang outside the fringes of your spread require tighter patterns and heavier pellets.

purely dimensional basis, but my observations indicate that there is a noteworthy advantage in 5s.

Many hunters place their decoys so that the farthest block is about 40 yards from the blind. This helps in judging range. However, birds over or just outside those extreme blocks require more energy than steel 4s and 5s can muster. For this range, a No. 2 skeet choke or modified comes in handy. Number 2 skeet (originally known as "skeet out") splits the difference between improved-cylinder and modified choke, having a 12-gauge bore constriction of about 0.015 to 0.016 inch, and it often patterns beautifully with the lighter steel pellets for 25- to 40-yard gunning.

For work over decoys 25 to 40 yards out, No. 3 steel shot has proven itself. Number 3s count 154 pellets to the ounce and carry about the same amount of energy as lead No. 5s. I can equate with them because lead 5s were my favorite duck load, except for the longest shots. A likely variant of the No. 3 loading is Remington's 1X3 "Duplex," which combines some steel 1s with the main mass of 3s for increased total pattern energy.

©CHUCK PETRIE

It's only decoy shooting when you can get them right over the blocks. The rest is pure and simple pass-shooting.

There are days when ducks won't drop into decoys no matter how expert the calling or how natural the spread. They'll hang outside the fringes and whistle overhead. These may be considered legitimate shots, but the open chokes and small shot sizes must go. Anything much beyond 35 yards becomes long range with steel shot, and tighter patterns and heavier pellets must prevail.

When selecting fine loads for open-choked 12s and decoy shooting, the heavier charges of $1\frac{1}{4}$ ounces in the standard-length hull and $1\frac{3}{8}$ ounces in the 3-inch case help to fill out the pattern. These heavier charges have lower published velocities by about 100 fps over the standard-length hull's $1\frac{1}{8}$-ouncer and the 3-inch 12's popular $1\frac{1}{4}$-ouncer. However, the velocity differential can be considered negligible over shorter distances. Multiple hits from sweetened pattern density are more important than sheer pellet velocity when skeet and improved-cylinder clusters are involved.

The 16- and 20-gauges can indeed be used for hunting over decoys. Either gauge will do. In fact, these trim, spirited pieces are delightful for close-in wingshooting. They are responsive, whereas some 12s will sit heavily in one's hands. But the hunter must remember that the shot charges from these smaller gauges are lighter. Hence, they don't offer as many pellets to fill out open patterns, and choke selection and self-discipline become vital factors.

Pellet sizes for the 16 and 20 can be pretty much the same as for the 12-gauge. Some of the best duck shooting I've done with the 3-inch 20 has been with No. 3s as mallards came in over the treetops lining a marshy area. These were from a gun bored modified and full. However, my patterning with the 1-ounce load of a 3-inch 20 indicates that improved-cylinder will give adequate density with No. 5s for 20- to 25-yard shooting as birds pitch into the decoys. But I like a stouter pellet, such as the steel 2 or 3 in the second barrel, for departing shots at longer ranges.

The 16-gauge's list of available steel shot sizes is limited, and if I couldn't get the desired 5s and 3s, I'd err in favor of the heavier 2s to make certain of adequate penetration at all legitimate ranges.

Sharp readers will note that steel No. 4s have not been mentioned here in glowing terms. I think steel 5s do a better job of sweetening open patterns at close range. Steel 3s retain adequate density while hitting harder than steel 4s. It might be argued that steel 4s are a compromise load for decoy hunting, but why use a compromise?

If you can get decoying action from ducks, and then control yourself to wait for them to cup their wings and come in...great! Use a skeet gun, an improved-cylinder, or a double bored improved-cylinder and modified with steel 5s, 3s, or Remington's Duplex 1X3 load. But if you can't lure them in, or if you find yourself unable to wait for the closest shots, be sure to take enough gun and load. It's only decoy shooting when you've got them right over the blocks. The rest is pure and simple pass shooting, and it takes tighter patterns and heavier shot to be effective well above the blind and out beyond the last bobbing block.

The 3½-inch 12-Gauge Magnum

A lthough the 10-gauge magnum's whopping hull is logically the best candidate for optimal steel-shot goose loads, not everyone can handle a massive 10-bore. This inspired the development of the 3½-inch 12-gauge magnum, which gives gunmakers the potential to build lighter, easier-handling 12-gauges chambered for a load almost as heavy as the 10's.

Browning BPS 12-Gauge Hunter

The strength of the 3½-inch 12 is its penchant for tight patterning. While its commercial 1⁹/₁₆-ounce steel loads do trail the 10-gauge magnum's charges by a few pellets, the 3½-inch 12's snug patterning characteristics tend to negate most of the load-weight differential. In my patterning, the 3½-inch 12 can generally equal, if not exceed, the performance of the 10.

chapter twelve

If a dour-faced judge rapped his gavel sternly and ordered me to make one goose-load recommendation for the 3½-inch 12, it would be the 1⁹⁄₁₆-ounce charge of steel Ts. In theory, steel Ts split the difference between the density of BBBs and the energy of steel Fs. And the theory works out in practice. A couple of years ago, my home state had more liberal goose limits than we'd seen in ages. I used a Benelli Super Black Eagle with a variety of 3½-inch 12-gauge

Remington Model 870 Super Magnum

loads. Every bird hit by Ts came down hard, whereas the lighter steel-shot sizes didn't show the same killing efficiency on the geese.

An interesting thing about the 3½-inch 12 and coarse steel shot such as BBBs, Ts, TTs, and Fs is that it delivers tight, full-choke patterns with just moderate-choke constrictions. It hammers patterning sheets with 75 to 80 percent patterns using just an improved-cylinder or modified choke tube. The same performance is claimed for other gauges and shorter 12-gauge rounds, too, but I've not seen it happen on paper as reliably and as consistently as it does with the 3½-inch 12s.

The 3½-inch 12-gauge magnum, then, has something going for it as a special goose gun when it's stuffed with heavy steel shot. Naturally tight shooting, it can perform cleanly at least as far as a typical hunter's skills can justify shooting.

How Much from the 3-Inch 20-Gauge?

Although there were some experiments with 3-inch 20-gauge loads before World War I, the project moved slowly because the right progressive-burning powders weren't available. This technology was developing during the 1930s, and Winchester was working on the 3-inch 20 only to be frustrated by World War II. In fact, it wasn't until well after the Second World War that the 3-inch 20-gauge case finally became available with a 1¼-ounce load of lead shot.

When the 1¼-ounce, 3-inch 20-gauge magnum load did finally hit the market, it practically killed off the 16-gauge. The 20 had become an all-round shotgun. Its 1¼-ounce loading didn't have the same velocity as the 1¼-ounce high-velocity 12-gauge load, running a published velocity of 1,185 feet per second against the 12's swifter 1,330 feet per second. However, a well-placed pattern from the 20-gauge magnum generally brought matters to a quick climax.

And then along came steel shot, apparently to ruin the 20-gauge magnum's heyday. It took years for the industry to put a 3-inch 20-gauge steel-shot magnum load on the market after the first 12-gauge steel-shot ammo was announced. The problem again was the "flow" factor, as steel shot doesn't compress and needs to be moved smoothly from chamber to bore. The high chamber pressures of lead-shot powders wouldn't do.

When the first steel loads for the 3-inch 20 came along, they held but 1 ounce of shot. No longer did this match the 12-gauge's payload. And that was only the beginning of the problem.

For the 3-inch 20's hull is full to the brim with the 1-ounce load only if there's nothing larger than No. 2 shot. The bulkier pellet sizes that one would select for high ducks or geese—the No. 1s, BBs, BBBs, and Ts—won't fit for a full ounce. There's too much wasted air space among such larger sizes. This isn't to say that steel No. 1s, BBs, BBBs, and Ts can't be shot from the 3-inch 20. It's just that those loads would be under an ounce, meaning the patterns would be sort of dicey. There is no guarantee of multiple hits with light charges of heavy pellets.

Remington 870 Express Youth 20-Gauge

So what do we do about the 3-inch 20 when it comes to waterfowling? The best answer is that we should use some intelligence and not overrate the round. It can still be used effectively for some selective situations, such as close- and moderate-range shooting over decoys. I've had excellent results with it on woodies in flooded timber where the flighting is fast and twisty but the distances aren't more than 30 to 35 yards. Indeed, the 20's forte is still its handling ease and speed, not long-range hitting power.

But it is pathetic to watch hunters pepper away at high geese and mallards with a steel-loaded 20 holding nothing more than No. 2s. For the steel No. 2 is already a marginal pellet on geese and big ducks beyond 40 yards, and to be pushing them farther is asking for crippled and lost birds. Bluntly stated, there are no truly efficient 20-gauge steel-shot loads for geese and high ducks on today's market. I shake my head sadly whenever I trudge the periphery of a goose refuge and find 20-gauge empties with No. 4 steel shot. And steel No. 3s are no better when the birds are high.

The father who buys his son a 20-gauge and has him blast at waterfowl with steel No. 2s, 3s, or 4s isn't doing the sport any favors. The 20's pattern simply doesn't pack the energy needed for clean knockdowns and positive retrieves as the range approaches and exceeds 40 yards. If the lad, or the father himself, is going to snipe at high waterfowl, a lightweight 12-gauge with standard-length loads pushing BBs or No. 1s is a better choice when less gun weight is desired.

Anyway you look at it, the switch to steel shot set the 3-inch 20-gauge magnum back at least 15 yards in effective range. Use it sparingly and intelligently on waterfowl.

Full-Choke Steel

S top in any gun shop these days, ask about the performance of steel shot, and you'll probably hear a half-dozen different voices claiming that full-choke barrels are taboo. Popular mythology nowadays maintains that the more open degrees of choke—improved-cylinder and modified, especially modified—are required with steel loads.

I beg to differ.

And I'm not just an argumentative iconoclast, either. I've shot up rolls of kraft wrapping paper since steel shot came along, and I know better because I've actually seen what full choke can do with steel loads. It ain't all bad, folks.

Let's begin with two important points. First, each gun-load duo is a physical law unto itself. Individual differences prevail. The only way to know exactly what a certain combo is doing is to test, but not many typical hunters want to do this. Most simply want to grab a gun, buy some shells, and be off. Unfortunately, you can't guess the pattern that'll come from any gun, nor can your gunsmith or sport shop clerk. And how many sport shop clerks have you seen out patterning lately?

©GARY KRAMER

Contrary to popular opinion, full choke and the right steel load can be just the ticket for long-range shots.

Second, and far more important, we must realize that the shooting industry's recommendations for chokes looser than full weren't predicated solely on patterning. A major reason for the industry's slant toward modified choke was to minimize the potential for gun damage (mainly ring bulging near the muzzle) when steel shot like BBs, BBBs, Ts, and Fs are sent through tightly choked barrels. These bulky spheres have horrible "flow" characteristics, meaning they don't shift about fluidly within their masses as they race from chamber to exit. Instead, they wedge against each other and take on the properties of a sluglike mass as they ram into the choke constriction, their combined energies sufficient to cause a ring bulge where the choke segment of the barrel begins to narrow.

Remington SP-10 Magnum

In general, the smaller sizes of steel shot such as 1s, 2s, 3s, 4s have not been inclined to do any such thing. These pellets have smoother flow qualities and, generally, squeeze down within their masses to flow more fluidly through the choke taper. But since the industry people know that hunters can be casually indifferent to the ammunition they shove through their guns, the gun gurus opted to publicize advice that was on the safe side. Hence comments tended to slant to open-bored guns—until just lately.

What has happened recently to change things? American gunmakers have made some technological advances, and we've suddenly got hard full-choke tubes that can handle the stresses of BBs, BBBs, Ts, and Fs. Use those special choke tubes, and you've got no real worries about linking steel shot with full choke.

And just how do full chokes and steel shot get along vis-á-vis patterning? In any number of instances, just fine, thank you! But I must stress that ultra-tight patterns aren't automatic, nor are they universal, when steel shot and full choke combine. We've got to respect that above-mentioned physical law of individual differences. In certain instances, full choke won't pattern any tighter than modified choke with a given load.

But when a full choke and a steel load take kindly to each other, they produce some thrilling results. Awhile back I used the Remington SP-10 Magnum with Remington Duplex steel loads of TxBB, and I patterned this tandem at 40 yards with every steel shot tube Remington included in the SP-10 package. The modified "REM" choke tube did 71 percent over 40 yards, which is basically in the low range of full choke (a full choke is expected to put 70 percent or more of its original shot charge into a 30-inch-diameter circle at 40 yards). However, when I screwed in the full-choke tube, that same SP-10 vaulted to over 90 percent for five consecutive patterns. This certainly knocks the idea about always using the more open chokes with steel shot into a cocked hat!

This work with the Remington SP-10 bolsters the evidence I've compiled thus far using other full-choked guns and various loads—namely, that although modified (and sometimes even improved-cylinder) chokes did sometimes reach above the 70 percent full-choke level with steel shot, the truly spectacular steel-shot patterns for long-range gunning came from bona fide full chokes. It doesn't happen with every choke-load pairing, as I've mentioned above, but it can be amazing when everything jibes.

Although there is a popular belief that improved-cylinder blends nicely with steel shot, I've never had improved-cylinders come close to giving the tightest clusters. In general, in fact, improved-cylinder will tend to scatter the smaller steel pellets like 4s, 3s, 2s and 1s in a manner similar to the way it handles lead shot, except that improved-cylinder leaves a greater center density with steel than with lead.

There is indeed a place for full choke in steel-shot usage: when the hunter wants to develop the tightest possible pattern with large pellets for long-range shots. But the right choke-load combination must be established scientifically by patterning, not by gun shop guesstimates.

Choking On Steel Shot?
Follow This Advice

Matching the choke and load was so much simpler when lead shot was universal. We could take almost any shot size, shoot it through a given degree of choke, and expect the pattern to be reasonably close to the anticipated spread and density. An improved-cylinder barrel, for example, would generally throw wider patterns with everything from skeet No. 9s to high-velocity No. 4s or BBs.

True, there would be some pattern variations even with lead shot. As I've said before, each gun-load combination is a physical law unto itself. But normally the variations would be within the parameters of each choke's accepted range of patterning efficiency, which is a leeway of roughly 10 percentage points. The above-mentioned improved-cylinder, for instance, is made to put 45 to 55 percent of its original load of lead pellets into a 30-inch circle at 40 yards.

But a given degree of choke no longer handles all sizes of steel shot for about the same patterns. Matching the load to the choke is more complicated with steel. Choke selection for steel shot depends on pellet size. If there is a rule of thumb, it is that the larger sizes of steel relate to the looser choke, whereas the smaller sizes respond more like lead shot and can still use the tighter degrees of choke. All of this is contrary to the bland advice of armchair experts who say "open your chokes for steel," because not all sizes of steel perform alike.

My patterning indicates that the smaller sizes, from steel No. 2s to No. 8s, will give more open patterns from skeet and improved-cylinder chokes, and that they'll often deliver basic modified-choke percentages from modified choke tubes. They don't automatically tighten to full choke from such open-choke tubes.

On the other hand, the larger steel pellets, from No. 1s and BBs to Fs, will frequently give full-choke percentages from modified chokes. In the 3½-inch 12-gauge super magnum, the same big goose pellets will tend to print tight patterns from just an improved-cylinder (about .01 inch constriction). But steel No. 4s from the same improved-cylinder choke tube will spread more liberally.

I'm beginning to believe that we should drop the old lead-shot designations (i.e., modified, full, etc.) for steel shot and proceed solely by choke dimensions. For example, here are my choke-tube suggestions for the 12-gauge (standard and 3-inch 12-gauge magnum only).

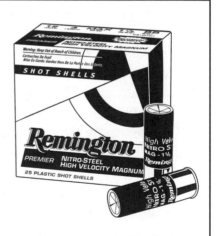

STEEL SHOT SIZES: 2 THROUGH 8

Range	Choke Constriction (in inches)
Close	.005
Moderate	.015–.020
Long	.030–.035

STEEL SHOT SIZES: 1 THROUGH F

Close	.000
Moderate	.005–.010
Long	.020–.030

Beware of
Choke-Tube Confusion

Most hunters today want a screw-in choke-tube feature on their shotguns for versatility, and in theory that's just fine. But in reality, the choke-tube situation has become a can of worms, and hunters would do well to recognize the potential for confusion.

For example, there are some tubes that extend well beyond the muzzle by an inch or more. Some of these are for steel shot; the added length takes the stress of steel-shot passage away from the barrel to minimize chances for ring bulging at the choke.

Then there are other extended tubes for lead shot only. These are called turkey tubes, or extra-full turkey tubes, and they are elongated so that a lengthy, gradual choke taper can be worked in for optimal pattern density. These should not be used with steel shot because their constrictions are too snug and they generally are not hardened.

The advent of overbored barrels has brought on a new generation of equally oversized choke tubes, such as the Browning Invector-Plus. These aren't only needed to fit the oversized bore, but also to balance choke constriction with the expanded bore diameter.

Adding to the dilemma are sets of choke tubes that are marked for one degree of choke with lead shot and another for steel shot. For example, on my desk is a tube stamped: MOD-LEAD, FULL-

STEEL. This is becoming increasingly common, as hunters want to know which patterns they'll get from which ammunition.

Perhaps the most frustrating situation today is the many different dimensions we'll find in choke tubes. Nasty fellow that I am, I frequently take an interior dial micrometer to chokes, and I find that the constrictions of factory-supplied tubes have been loosened considerably. Whereas the standard for 12-gauge lead-shot full chokes was once .040 inch, with .035 inch being a loose full choke, I have recently measured some designated full-choke tubes to find no more than .025 inch constriction. That's barely improved-modified, and on paper they didn't come close to full-choke percentages with premium buffered loads.

I also have a pair of factory-supplied modified tubes that measure out to barely .01 inch, which is roughly tight improved-cylinder. They don't pattern to honest modified choke either, holding instead to a basic improved-cylinder.

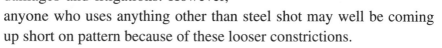

What's happening? I suspect that gunmakers have gotten spooked about the public's indiscretions with steel shot and have loosened the chokes overall to avoid damages and litigations. However, anyone who uses anything other than steel shot may well be coming up short on pattern because of these looser constrictions.

Can you avoid choke-tube confusion? Only if you take your choke tube to a machinist or gunsmith and have him measure the constriction and compare it to your gun's main bore diameter. Sorry about that, but don't blame me. I didn't do it.

Do We Still Have a
Long-Range Duck Gun?

It's quite common these days to hear that steel shot has virtually negated long-range duck shooting. The popular press has published the results of tests that indicate that steel loads are cripplers, thanks to the way air resistance slows steel pellets and quickly reduces their energy.

But as I stood on a hillock rimming the south end of a marsh one evening, limit of mallards in hand, I couldn't help but ponder the veracity of those widespread generalizations. Readings from a range finder indicated that that evening's flight was topping the rise at 45 to 55 yards, and both of my birds had been cleanly taken. I repeated the performance the next evening, again doing so without a lost cripple.

My ammunition on that occasion was Remington's 12-gauge 3-inch, 1¼-ounce loading of steel BBs. The gun was a work-worn Remington Model 1100 with a 28-inch, modified-choked barrel. Actual patterning, not armchair guesswork, had shown it to be throwing patterns of 80 to 83 percent at 40 yards.

Although few duck hunters thought in terms of BBs during the days of lead shot, it is now a potent pellet for long-range ducks when the choke-load combination delivers tight patterns, for the steel BB overcomes air resistance better than steel No. 2s and retains more energy beyond 40 to 45 yards. Couple that penetrating power with a high density, and one has the ingredients for 50- to 55-yard duck shooting.

There are approximately 50 pellets in an ounce of lead BBs, while an ounce of steel BBs contains 70 to 72 pellets. The added 20 to 22 pellets per ounce of steel BBs obviously increases the potential for greater pattern density, which in turn promises multiple hits. If we carry pellet counts further, we find 62 to 63 lead BBs in a 1$\frac{1}{4}$-ounce charge, while steel BBs count to 88 to 89 for the same charge weight. That's an advantage of about 25 pellets in the 1$\frac{1}{4}$-ounce load, and in an 80 percent pattern it bolsters the density by about 20 pellets, which is hardly insignificant.

Another reason for using steel BBs for long-range duck shooting is pattern retention. Experiments have shown that patterns of steel shot tend to deteriorate faster beyond 40 yards than those of lead charges. Why? Because the steel pellets, being lighter than lead of the same size, are more readily affected by air resistance as their

©BILL BUCKLEY

With the right firepower, birds can still be taken beyond 45 yards—if you can put the pattern in place.

velocities drop. However, my experiments indicate that pattern breakdown is less emphatic with the heavier BBs, BBBs, and Ts. These larger spheres simply pack more energy to hold their own a little longer against air resistance. On a retained percentage basis, steel BBs outshoot steel 4s and 2s at 50 to 60 yards.

There is room to argue that steel No. 1s are also excellent pellets at 40 to 50 yards. But my own observations are that steel 1s won't do anything steel BBs can't do a little better beyond 40 yards when patterns are snug.

Therein lies an important factor in long-range duck shooting with any type of pellet—the pattern. Popular mythology aside, I have not gotten my best patterns with steel BBs using skeet or improved-cylinder choke—as is so often recommended by experts who sit in barber chairs. Modified and improved-modified chokes have always patterned better, in my experience. I know my readership hates to read this next statement, but it is the hunter's responsibility to match the choke to the load for optimal pattern density. Patterns do vary as chokes and loads are interchanged, and crippling hits at long range are often the result of pattern weaknesses due to choke-load mismatches.

Thus we still do have some long-range capabilities despite the age of steel in waterfowling. Tight patterns of steel BBs from 10- or 12-gauge magnum loads can handle 55 to 60 yards with surprising effectiveness—if you can put the pattern in place.

Steel Shot and the Side-by-Each

The romance of modern waterfowling is often embodied in the guns of yesteryear. Hunters who aren't simply interested in piling up bag limits often get a kick—both emotionally and physically—from using smoothbores that stroked the skies in the "good ol' days." It's a matter of nostalgia...of enjoying the gun...of wanting to do something in a special way or not do it at all.

I have to admit that I'm one of said breed, a depraved shotgun nut who would sooner get just one bird with a gun that suddenly caught my fancy than fill a gunnysack using any other fowling stick at that moment. For those of us thus afflicted, the gun makes the hunt; we can enjoy even a bad day, because spice is added by that special piece of nostalgia.

At one time in America's hunting history, the dominant gun was a side-by-side double, often with big hammers jutting upward like a prairie jack's ears and a stock as crooked as your retriever's hind leg. Some of them are now legitimately cherished collector's items; others are pure clunkers that tend to be overvalued. But the point is that they did their share of waterfowling. Periodically, I've taken one or another of the golden oldies duck hunting for auld lang syne.

One of them was an Ithaca 10-bore double with fluid steel barrels, tall hammers, and a low-combed stock. It had a set of 30-inch barrels with 2⅞-inch chambers. I found it, sadly neglected, on a table at a gun show. Upon handling it I found I could swing it better than any 10-gauge I'd ever used. It went home with me, and to get the most from it I reloaded my own 2⅞-inch hulls with plastic wads and copper-plated shot. I'm glad no scorekeeper followed me through the marsh and my jump-shooting routes when I carried that gun. I'm lucky if I scored 50 percent with it. But it was great fun trying the upright shooting technique that prevailed when the Ithaca was in its prime.

Another time I used an Ansley H. Fox Grade B that had heavy, 30-inch barrels and 2½-inch chambers for which I also had to reload shorter shells. I wouldn't have minded at all if a scorekeeper had been

Alternatives to steel shot, like tungsten (above) and bismuth, are good, effective choices for waterfowlers who like to hunt with classic side-by-sides.

around then, for the Fox had a higher comb and I shot it fairly well in high-angle fire.

Today's tragedy is, of course, that the side-by-eaches of yesteryear are not totally compatible with steel shot. Consequently, we are somewhat deprived of the fun of using them for duck or goose hunting unless we are willing to accept the potential of gun damage. In general, the thin barrels of those early days could be ring-bulged by masses of steel hammering into the choke constriction. Then there is the possibility of barrel and rib loosening under the stresses of steel shot because those parts were generally soft soldered rather than brazed.

This doesn't mean that a sportsman who loves double barrels, especially the horizontal kind, need forgo his pleasures. There are side-by-sides around that will handle steel—they've been built for the purpose. Don't expect to find them on a Kmart bargain counter, of course. But if you cherish nice side-by-sides, you're still alive.

Some of the first doubles made and advertised for steel shot were Winchester's Model 23 Heavy Duck Gun, a 12-gauge side-by-side; and the same model in 20-gauge, designated the Light Duck Gun. These are still around on the used gun or collector's market, many of them still new and in the box. I used the 20-gauge model, complete with choke tubes. If there has ever been a finer finished gun in its price range, I'd love to see it. The repro Parker comes dear, monetarily speaking, but so does one of the originals, which isn't toughened for steel shot.

Another gun made with steel shot in mind is the Classic Doubles Model 201, which is an upgraded variant of the Winchester Model 23. Although now defunct, Classic Doubles built the Model 201 with brazed barrels, chrome lining, and elongated forcing cones. It has the long, Parker-like beavertail forearm and fancy walnut, and those with improved-cylinder and modified chokes tend to pattern quite nicely with steel loads.

On the lower-priced end, Savage once made a Model 311 Waterfowler with 28-inch barrels choked for steel shot. Savage had financial woes, however, and is now attempting a comeback. Whether the Model 311 steel-shot-compatible side-by-side will be put back into the line has not been announced as of this writing.

©BILL BUCKLEY

Some waterfowlers get a special kick—both emotionally and physically—
from swinging old doubles like the Winchester Model 21 pictured above.

The people at American Arms, Inc., have brought in a 10-gauge
magnum side-by-side that is openly recommended for steel shot, and
it doesn't cost an arm and a leg.

One of the nicer production-grade side-by-sides was the
Browning B-SS, some of which are still showing up at gun shops in
used but excellent condition. Gun trading tabloids also run classified
ads offering B-SS guns that are still new and in their original boxes.
Not all B-SS guns were made for steel shot, but Browning's letter on
the subject states that all Browning sporting arms manufactured after
1975 and stamped "Made in Japan" with conventional fixed chokes
can handle steel-shot cartridges except those loaded with BBs, BBBs,
Ts, and Fs. This leaves plenty of room for steel No. 2s and 1s for
waterfowl, plus the lighter sizes for upland usage if and when
necessary.

How do you know if a B-SS was made after 1975? Browning
reports that nearly all guns made thereafter have two letters to

indicate the year of manufacture. Browning's code runs like this: M=0, Z=1, Y=2, X=3, V=5, T=6, R=7, P=8, and N=9. Put "PT" together, and one has 1986; "PR" means 1987, etc.

Waterfowlers who hate to give up on the side-by-side needn't do so just because we've entered the age of steel. Some horizontal guns can take it.

Shotshell Velocities

L et's say the duck season starts a couple weeks down the line, and you've just picked up a box of 12-gauge target loads to have a go at some skeet clays to get the ol' swing back. You look at the data line printed on the box, and it says it's a 3-drams-equivalent load with $1\frac{1}{8}$ ounces of No. 9 shot. What the heck does "3 drams equivalent" mean? Come to think of it, you've bought a lot of shotshells before, and you've seen other drams-equivalent markings. What are those numbers all about?

Essentially, the drams-equivalent number concerns each respective load's velocity. It has absolutely nothing to do with the specific weight of the powder charge in any modern smokeless-powder load. Nothing. The key word is "equivalent," and it does nothing more than indicate a velocity comparison between the black-powder loads of yesteryear and the modern stuff of today. So don't for a split instant believe that shotshells marked "3 drams equivalent" have an honest 3 drams of powder in them!

The inception of the drams-equivalent term dates to that transitional period nearly 100 years ago when smokeless powder was replacing black powder. People then had a pretty good idea what a given charge of black powder could do, but how could they equate those performances with that of the newer smokeless stuff? The

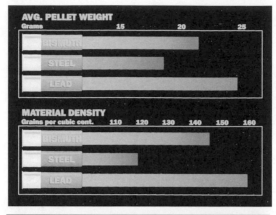

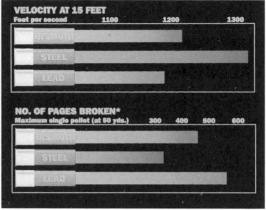

answer was the drams-equivalent marking on smokeless shotshells, which, succinctly stated, means that load of smokeless powder will generate the same approximate velocity as was once delivered by a given dram-measured charge of black powder with a certain shot charge.

At one time, for example, it was found that a 3-dram charge of black powder would drive a 1¹/₈-ounce load of lead shot to about 1,200 feet per second. When smokeless powder came along, those 1¹/₈-ounce shot charges, which left the muzzle around 1,200 fps, were listed as the equivalent of 3 drams of black powder. Hence, they have become known as 3-drams-equivalent loads, and they are today our so-called "heavy" trap, skeet, and sporting clays ammo.

You may have noticed that steel-shot loads generally do not have a drams-equivalent rating other than the term "max." That's because there is no way to equate black-powder performances with steel shot; steel was never used in the days of yore. And since steel shot has an entirely different "flow factor" than lead shot, our steel ammo sets its own pace. The term "max" on steel loads just means that the load is doing the top allowable velocities for its chamber pressure. To learn exactly what these velocities are, you'll have to read manufacturers' catalogs.

When reading up on velocities, do remember that the published data are not muzzle velocities. Shot loads are clocked at a distance of three feet from the muzzle. Moreover, the industry's equipment doesn't check the leading pellets but rather gives the average of the entire shot string as it passes through coil chronograph screens. (Amateur handloader-type chronographs, on the other hand, trigger on the leading pellet; consequently, handloaders will not get the same readings as the industry, which triggers en mass.)

Thus it is wrong to believe that the published shotshell data is muzzle velocity. It is 30-foot coil velocity.

Why make such a big point of that? Because research by Ed Lowry, a former Winchester ballistician, indicates that considerable velocity is lost in the first three to four feet of free flight when pellets encounter air resistance (drag). By using sensitive equipment and calculations, Lowry found that it takes a muzzle velocity of roughly 1,300 fps to record a velocity of 1,200 fps at three feet with lead No. 7$^{1}/_{2}$s. Thus the typical 3-drams-equivalent trap load mentioned above may have a published velocity of 1,200 fps, but it's actually leaving the muzzle at 1,300 fps!

The same velocity loss is true for steel loads, only more so. Lowry's work shows that a load of steel BBs with a published velocity of 1,350 fps must actually be driven to 1,459 fps at the muzzle. Because steel shot is light, it loses velocity to air drag rather quickly, in this case about 110 fps in just three to four feet. Luckily, air resistance works less violently against slower-moving shot than it does against high-speed pellets, so that the velocity loss diminishes as the shot string gets farther out.

How Waterfowl Loads Changed with the Times

Although a casual look back would have one believe that brass cases were the immediate forerunners of our modern paper and plastic shotshells, there were already paper cartridges around in the middle of the nineteenth century. The first successful break-action, breechloading double was developed by a Frenchman and shown, along with paper-cased loads, in 1851 at the Great Exhibition in London.

Despite the early availability of paper shotshells in Europe and England, however, many waterfowlers of that era favored the all-brass cases because they were impervious to moisture and swelling. Moreover, paper cases weren't always readily available in the United States. Certain experiments were also tried with cases made of zinc, and other tests have been conducted with aluminum, but neither of these metals proved as satisfactory as brass, especially among those who reloaded.

Technological advances during the late nineteenth century and early twentieth century brought ammunition manufacturers to focus on paper cases. Brass rounds did not feed reliably through the tubular-magazined repeaters that were coming into vogue, and a wax impregnating process did much to waterproof paper tubes and eliminate the old complaints about their swelling and potential misfires in damp environs. In addition, new production practices reduced the cost of making paper hulls, and experiments with folded crimps indicated that they formed better seals against moisture than did the original roll crimps.

As smokeless powders were applied to paper shotshells, it was learned that their higher gas pressures found a weak spot where the paper and metal joined at the bottom of the case. Consequently, early manufacturers used a higher base wad on the more powerful loadings, with an accompanying higher exterior brass head to support the paper. This high brass is no longer needed on plastic cases, but manufacturers continue to use them because waterfowlers believe that high brass means high velocity. In most respects, the high brass has become an anachronism. But tradition is a potent factor.

The main improvement in shotshells after World War I was not in the case itself but rather in the powders, which became slower burning and made it possible to shoot heavier charges at higher velocities. This was when the famous $3^3/_4$-drams-equivalent, $1^1/_4$-ounce 12-gauge duck

©CHRIS DORSEY

Shotshells have come a long way since the early days of brass and paper casings and fast-burning powders—but nothing can beat the artwork on the old boxes.

load came along to drive its pattern at the published velocity of 1,330 feet per second. Some ammunition makers advertised long and loud that the progressive-burning powders produced shorter, more effective shot strings because fewer pellets were deformed by firing setback. Winchester-Western Super-X and Super-Speed loads, along with Remington's Nitro Express, are cases in point.

The same slow-burning powders inspired experimentation with extra-length shotshells, such as the 3½-inch 10-gauge magnum and the 3-inch 12- and 20-gauge magnums. But that's another part of waterfowling history.

Moisture-Proofing Steel Loads

Moisture has always plagued waterfowlers. It made a mockery of ignition in flintlocks and continued to be a frustration even when percussion caps came into vogue during the nineteenth century. Nor was the self-contained, papercased shotshell a perfect seal; moisture still penetrated to make the filler wads swell so much that they sometimes wouldn't chamber. Problems didn't disappear with plastic-cased steel-shot loads either. More than a few marshland hunters can tell stories about triggering "bloopers" with a flock of mallards over the decoys.

America's major shotshell makers—Federal, Winchester, and Remington—have taken a hard look at improved moisture proofing. Both Winchester and Remington have adopted new steps for eliminating load malfunctions.

Winchester's concept is based on an internal seal, and loads so assembled will be printed with the "Drylok" tradename. The seal is actually built on a two-piece wad system that begins with a short overpowder cup with an H-type configuration, meaning that it has flanges extending in both directions, downward to seal the powder gases and forward to seal out whatever moisture might seep in through the crimp. A typically long, hard, plastic shotcup fits into the upper portion of the overpowder cup to force the leading edges of the H-type wad tightly against the interior hull wall.

Does this two-part wad work? I was in on an experiment that indicates that it does. While hunting near Stuttgart, Arkansas, we immersed several boxes of the new Drylok loads and let them soak overnight. The next morning we used them on mallards in the flooded oaks without having any misfires or bloopers—and we did take limits, so the loads were indeed effective.

Remington's approach to moisture proofing focuses on the exterior of the case rather than the interior. Tests run by Remington indicated that moisture can sneak through the primer pocket and cause trouble, so they are sealing both the primer pocket and the crimp with a lacquer tagged "Wet Proof." These Remington steel-shot loads will be sold under the Nitro Steel and Nitro Express brand names, and the lacquer around the primer should be obvious. Remington will use new packaging for these loads with the Wet Proof designation clearly marked on the box. It's encouraging to see that manufacturers have addressed hunters' concerns for improved steel-shotshell performance.

Today's plastic leak-proof shotshells have virtually put an end to moisture-induced misfires and bloopers.

The Basics of Backboring

Prior to the advent of precision measuring equipment, the bore diameters of shotguns were determined by the number of round lead balls of a specific diameter needed to make a pound. If a one-ounce lead ball fit a given bore, it was known as a 16-gauge, because there are 16 ounces in a pound. When a lead ball weighing one-twelfth of a pound (1.33 ounces) fit a given bore, the shotgun became known as a 12-gauge.

When measuring devices were invented, the industry continued to use the same dimensions developed during the lead ball days, but established standardized specs for each gauge. Those industry standards prevail today.

The standard bore dimensions were developed during the black-powder era, when shot charges were relatively light. Ten-gauge shotshells, for example, were often loaded with just 1¼ ounces of shot, while 12-gauge rounds were commonly topped by 1⅛-ounce charges. When heavier shot charges were used, pellet velocities generally declined because the older shotguns couldn't handle the chamber pressures needed to drive magnum loads to high velocities.

Although some barrelsmiths tinkered with bore diameters and tapers during the black-powder era, the concept of "overboring" didn't become popular until the advent of improved smokeless

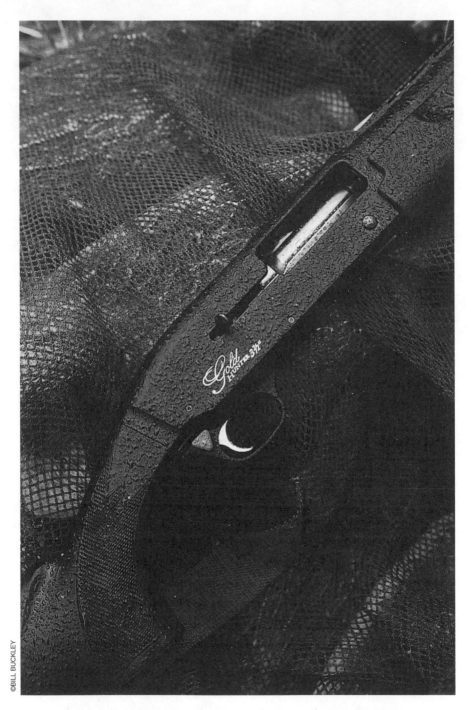

chapter twenty-two

©BILL BUCKLEY

Browning's semi-automatic Gold Hunter comes with an overbored barrel that allows for the smoother passage of magnum shot charges.

powders between the world wars. Known as progressive-burning propellants, these powders permitted the use of heavier shot charges.

Progressive-burning powders led to the development of new magnum shotshells, including the 3½-inch 10-gauge magnum, the 3-inch 12-gauge magnum, and the 3-inch 20-gauge magnum. When the heavier and longer shot charges didn't provide optimal patterning and velocity, gunmakers began to question the effectiveness of the old bore-diameter standards. Consequently, barrelsmiths began building shotguns with various oversized bore diameters designed to fire the new magnum loads.

One of the foremost practitioners of overboring was Burt Becker of the Philadelphia-based A. H. Fox Gun Company. His overbored Fox doubles were made famous in the hands of the legendary outdoor writer Nash Buckingham, who was widely regarded as the greatest wingshot of his generation. Although Buckingham's guns were customized by Becker, the overbore concept went commercial with the development of the Super-Fox, alias the HE Grade Fox. Today these fowling pieces are treasured collectibles.

Overbored barrels were not widely accepted by shotgunners until the 1970s, when plastic wads and their gas-sealing overpowder cups were invented, which dramatically improved the efficiency of overbored barrels. Seattle barrelsmith Stan Baker helped popularize the concept by coining the term "backboring" as a synonym for overboring, because he felt the prefix "over" fed skepticism.

In recent years, overbored shotgun barrels, alias backbored barrels, have become popular with clay shooters and, to a lesser extent, hunters. Mossberg has been a leader in the field; its Model 835 Ulti-Mag is overbored for enhanced ballistics and patterning with 3½-inch 12-gauge magnum loads. Ruger also builds its over-unders with overbored barrels, and Browning has begun using them on some field guns, such as their semi-automatic Gold Hunter.

So what are the advantages of overbores to the modern shotgunner? When matched to a lengthened forcing cone, the relaxed dimensions of overbores allow a smoother passage of the shot charge, which, in turn, improves patterning, reduces friction for higher velocity, and can lower recoil (depending on the actual load and bore diameter). Given their many attributes, overbored shotgun barrels may well become the wave of the future. And I, for one, would like to see the concept expanded to include the smaller gauges as well.

©GARY R. ZAHM

s h o o t i n g

"

Do it like a hunter: mount, point, shoot —now!
— Don Zutz —

"

Twenty Tips For
Successful Wingshooting

Successful wingshooting, like success at anything else, is the result of little things that come together at the right time. The twenty tips listed below are some of those "little things." Taken seriously, and practiced or expanded on, they can improve a waterfowler's results afield and ensure more clean hits for positive retrieves.

SHOTSHELLS

1. Study catalog ammunition listings to learn which steel-shot loads have the highest velocities. Steel pellets can use every advantage, no matter how minor.

2. In cold weather, keep some loads close to body heat. Steel-shot loads have slow-burning powders that will ignite better when kept warm.

3. Don't guess at a load's performance. Do some actual patterning at the range to make absolutely certain that the gun-load pairing is giving you the density needed for clean kills.

SHOTGUNS

4. Be critical of stock fit. In shotgunning, the shooter's eye positioned squarely atop the comb acts as a rear sight. If the comb

dimensions don't permit this proper eye location during the swing, misalignment will occur. When a shotgunner's onside eye isn't correctly positioned, it's tantamount to a rifle's rear sight being knocked out of adjustment.

5.   Make certain a gun fits when you're wearing your heaviest hunting clothes. Too often a gun that fits on a summer evening while you're shopping in a sports shirt turns out to be too long when you're bundled in late-season garb. One trick is having two different recoil pads fitted to the same gun: a full-sized pad for early season and light clothing, and a lesser pad for late season.

6.   Be skeptical of the advice to use open-choked guns for steel shot. Contrary to public generalizations, open chokes do not automatically give tight patterns with all steel loads. The industry's reason for advocating open chokes in the past was mainly to eliminate the potential for ring bulging full-choked barrels. However, now that the industry has developed full-choke tubes that will withstand the stress of steel-shot passage, full choke is again a legitimate part of wingshooting. And despite popular fictions, full choke will still deliver the tightest patterns in shotgunning. As a rule of thumb, open-choked shotguns will give their tightest patterns with the heaviest pellets, such as BBs, BBBs, Ts, and Fs, while often opening to wider clusters with the lighter steel pellets. Here again, it's an individual matter, and a hunter must pattern to learn what his equipment is doing with each load.

SHOOTING TECHNIQUE

7.   Don't aim—point and swing! The shotgun is a dynamic, short-range piece that is made to be pointed and swung, not held steadily and aimed like a rifle. A hunter who persists in lining up the beads on his shotgun, or who uses a ventilated rib like a sighting device, is doing it all wrong. In some respects, the beads and ribs of hunting guns are unnecessary and serve only to mislead shooters. The essence of wingshooting is based on hand-eye coordination with absolutely minimal visual contact with the gun.

8.   Focus sharply on the leading edge of the target. The human eyes cannot focus clearly on objects both near and far. They must be

focused on the target to optimize hand-eye coordination relative to the bird. If the shooter's eyes are aware of the gun, it should be seen only as a fuzzy, out-of-focus blur. Natural coordination should establish enough pointing accuracy to get the pattern on target, provided the forward allowance is correct.

9. Don't be overly concerned if rain pelts against your shooting glasses. It's difficult to believe, but clay-target shooters have learned that you can see the target sharply by focusing on it through the drops. Rubbing the lenses in continual attempts to clear them only smears the glass and makes things worse.

10. Use shoulder and body pivot to swing the gun. This complete pivot keeps your head in place so that the eye is always properly positioned for accurate alignment. If the gun is moved solely by hand action, it will be pulled or pushed away from the eye and lose accuracy.

11. Many expert field shots eventually learn that they do better to keep their guns down until a bird comes within range than they do by mounting at the first sight of a target. By mounting only when the

©BILL BUCKLEY

Keep your head down and your master eye placed squarely atop the comb. There will be plenty of time to see the results after the shooting's done.

target is in range, you gain use of the gun's momentum for a smooth, accelerating swing. Guns mounted too early induce the hunter to make a long, draggy tracking move.

12. Use as light a grip on your shotgun as you safely can to control it. Clenching the gun causes your arm and shoulder muscles to tighten, producing a stiff, jerky swing. Cut down on hand tension for a smooth, fluid swing.

13. Never skybust. But when you have a high bird in range, don't let it lull you into making slow swings or aiming deliberately. High birds present the optical illusion of flying slower than they really are traveling, with the result that hunters think they can merely pick a spot ahead of the target and aim a shot to that point. Millions of shots are missed because they lack a swing. You might feel odd when making a crisp swing through and well ahead of a high bird that appears to be standing still, but gun dynamics are needed.

14. Don't dwell on the trigger as you admire your forward allowance. Learn to use brisk trigger timing that fires the shot immediately when things feel rhythmic and right. Delaying trigger pull while you second-guess your lead takes away the instinctive hand-eye coordination you must develop for good wingshooting.

15. Always follow through. It is critical to maintain gun speed as the trigger is being pulled. Targets as high as geese and passing mallards or as fast as crossing teal and bluebills will cover considerable distances between the time a trigger is pulled and the time the shot charge is rushed up and out of the barrel. If the swing is stopped at trigger pull, the target will be long gone by the time the shot string arrives.

16. Keep your head down! In the excitement of field shooting, there is always temptation to lift your head and see the fine results of your shooting. A lifted head prevents alignment because it takes the master eye away from its necessary placement squarely atop the comb.

17. Learn to feel comfortable with increased swing speed. Most shots at flying targets are missed behind and/or below, the result of inadequate lead. To generate more forward allowance, the gun must be swung briskly. There is more to wingshooting than merely

tracking a target; the swing must be aggressive. There is no better place for a hunter to start improving his swing than on a skeet field.

18. Start your swing by coming from behind the target. Hunters who start ahead of the bird (sustained leading) often move too slowly or tend to stop their swing at trigger pull. By starting behind the target, however, you are forced to accelerate to build up a forward allowance. This acceleration generates gun momentum to help build longer leads and stretch them into positive follow-throughs.

19. Make certain of your footing whether you're in a blind, a pit, a boat, or hip-deep in the marsh. A steady base is needed for balance. A hunter without a secure base generally can't make an efficient pivot and is most likely a safety hazard.

20. Practice! The game of sporting clays has high-tower shots much like those taken in waterfowling. Good old-fashioned skeet shooting offers a lot of sound work in swinging on snappy targets. Too frequently, I'm afraid, hunters tend to believe that swinging on a game bird is different than swinging on a clay target, but that's not true. The same mount, swing, fire, and follow-through sequence is common to all shotgunning.

So there you have them—twenty tips for better wingshooting with an emphasis on waterfowling. Each tip could be a book chapter in itself. And the hunter who feels—indeed, knows—that his shooting leaves something to be desired, can easily extend his research by delving into the specialized books on these subjects as well as by getting acquainted at the local clay-target club.

Good luck, keep your head down, be smooth, and follow through!

©BILL BUCKLEY

Holding your shotgun with as light a grip as you safely can cuts down on hand tension and allows for a smooth, fluid swing.

chapter twenty-four

Point-and-Shoot Shotguns

Successful shotgun shooting has much in common with athletic skills that require sound hand-eye coordination. A baseball player, for example, doesn't make a deliberate attempt to line up his bat with the ball; he is coached to keep his eyes on the ball and to bring the bat to where his eyes are looking by natural coordination.

In like manner, classic wingshooting is predicated on the shooter keeping his eyes focused sharply on the moving target while his hands bring the gun into play without his ever looking back to establish alignment. If you're doing it right, you're not taking a squinty-eyed aim along the rib or lining up a couple of beads. We ignore all the precision sighting stuff in shotgunning by trusting the hands to line up the gun between our eye and the target.

Since the hands are so vital to good shooting, the best shotguns have design features that facilitate hand-eye coordination. The most important of these features are the gripping points. Such things as splinter forends and beavertail forearms, and straight (English-style), semi-pistol, and full-pistol grips are there for reasons other than appearances. The shotgun owner who says he wants a gun with a straight grip because it looks racy knows not whereof he speaks.

Shotguns are easier and more accurately pointed if their grip designs keep the shooter's hands working together on the same plane

©BILL BUCKLEY

Guns that keep the shooter's hands on the same plane will often be the most comfortable to point.

relative to the bore axis. Human hands tend to work better together when they are placed on the same level. Baseball bats and golf clubs, for instance, keep the player's hands in line nicely for efficient use. But can you imagine how much trouble a baseball player or golfer would have making solid, accurate contact if his bat or club had an offset handle that placed each hand on a different plane?

The same concept is true in shotgun design and use. The hands should be kept level. There are a pair of esoteric terms that describe ideal shotgun gripping for the most natural, fluid, accurate pointing: (1) hands-in-line arrangement, and (2) hands-to-bore relationship.

When we speak of the hands-in-line arrangement, we mean that the gripping points place both hands at the same depth below the bore axis. If we converted this to an illustration via plane geometry, the bore axis and gripping points would run as parallel lines. This is ideal, for if a shooter's hands aren't on the same plane, there is a natural tendency for them to fight back into alignment with each other, thus tilting the gun as it comes to bear.

Following the hands-in-line arrangement, guns with full-pistol grips normally have deep beavertail forearms; the beavertails lower the leading hand to place it on the same level as the trigger hand. Likewise, side-by-sides with the straight grip have splinter or slender, semi-beavertail forends, which elevate both hands relative to the bores so that the hands can work in tandem.

The hands-to-bore relationship implies that the closer the hands are to the bore axis, the more accurately they can be pointed by natural hand-eye coordination. If the hands go accurately to where the eye is looking, the bore that lies closest to the shooter's palms will obviously be "on." The classic British game gun follows these ideas with great detail, combining a straight grip with a minor splinter forend to keep the hands in line and as close to the bore axis as possible.

Does a shotgun need both of these gripping points designed to ultimate perfection before it points effectively? As a personal observation, I have come to believe that the hands-in-line arrangement seems eminently more important than the hands-to-bore relationship. The greatness of the British doubles notwithstanding, I can only say that there are some repeaters that are also quite natural pointers despite positioning the shooter's hands somewhat lower.

One of these is John M. Browning's Auto-5, which with its rather trim forend and semi-pistol grip put the hunter's hand on the same basic plane, albeit somewhat further below the bore axis than is the case with side-by-sides. So, too, did the Remington Model 1100 catch the public's fancy because of its natural pointing qualities, thanks to the way the deeper forearm places the shooter's leading hand in line with the trigger hand, which on an 1100 is lowered by the full-pistol grip.

Thus a shotgun's pointability isn't determined by such cosmetics as beads, matted receiver tops, ribs, or assorted bells and whistles. Pointability stems from the way a gun is gripped by the hands to harmonize with hand-eye coordination. Keep your hands in line, get a properly fitted stock, always focus sharply on the target—and you're on your way.

chapter twenty-five

Stock Fit and Nonsense

It is a common scene in gun shops and wherever shotguns are traded: The prospective buyer wraps his hand around a gun's wrist, then lays the stock along his forearm and works the butt into the crook of his elbow. If the gun snuggles up nicely as he forms his arm into a right angle, he proclaims it "a fit." If the stock comes up short or is so long that he can't make it jibe with his forearm, he sets the gun aside and says, "This one doesn't fit me!"

If there is anything farcical in shotgunning, it is this ridiculous practice of trying to judge stock fit by gauging its length against one's forearm. The length of one's forearm relative to a shotgun's stock has absolutely nothing to do with judging shotgun fit.

In theory, the shotgun stock is little more than a sight mount. Its purpose is to fill the space between a shooter's hands, cheekbone, and shoulder so that the onside eye can be placed squarely atop the comb for easy viewing over the receiver and to expedite eye-muzzle-target alignment. As has been written so often in the past (but not always appreciated or understood by many hunters), the eye becomes the rear sight of a shotgun. If the onside eye isn't solidly in place throughout the swing and follow-through, accurately pointing the shotgun is like shooting a rifle that's had its rear sight knocked out of adjustment. The eye must ride the shotgun's sight mount (the comb) for accurate shooting.

©CHRIS DORSEY

A proper-fitting gun will line up squarely against your cheek and shoulder and allow you to look immediately over the receiver and muzzle at the target.

Merely holding a shotgun's stock against one's forearm and relating it to the crook of the elbow tells nothing about how the eye will greet and rest on the comb. Stock length is a worthless measurement unless it also involves the location of the eye atop the comb. The point is that stock fit can only be ascertained when the gun is mounted to the shoulder and the shooter's head is in position. This test determines whether the eye will find the comb for proper alignment and target visibility.

If the comb height is correct for a given individual, he or she will be looking immediately over the receiver and muzzle at the target. Seeing the rib pitched upward means that the comb is too high; the shooter will be looking down at the rib or barrel and shooting will result in high pattern placement. On the other hand, the comb is too low if the shooter looks directly into his thumb or the rear of the receiver without seeing easily and comfortably over the gun. Indeed, something's very wrong if a hunter must jiggle his head about to attain horizontal or vertical alignment with the center of the receiver and muzzle. As with sighting-in a rifle, adjustments must be made on the shotgun "sight." This means finding a gun with different stock dimensions or custom fitting a new stock on an existing gun.

Gun fit is especially important in long-range shooting with tight patterns. If the eye is just slightly off center, the alignment error is magnified at 50 to 60 yards. The result is a crippling fringe hit or a clean miss. "It looked good to me," a hunter may say, but in reality there was enough eye-to-muzzle misalignment to cause a miss.

The most reliable way to check gun fit is by patterning. To do this, set up a one-yard-square sheet of cardboard at 45 to 50 yards and place a black aiming point in the center of the sheet. Then, while wearing hunting clothes, mount the gun, preferably one with a tight-patterning choke, and fire at the black mark with the same speed and timing you would use on game. Don't take time to wiggle into position as a bench-rest rifleman would. And don't take a squinty-eyed aim at the sheet. Do it like a hunter: mount, point, shoot—now! If your pattern isn't centered about the bull's-eye, you've got a problem.

Most often, that problem is a hunter's own failure to get his eye into position during the move-mount-shoot dynamics. Anyone who has time can work his head into position or slide the gun around, but how long will a mallard hover overhead waiting for a hunter to wiggle into position? How long will ruffed grouse hang in an opening in the pines? And how long do you have before a sharptail is out of range on a windy day? Not long. Do your patterning for accuracy under the same circumstances required when you shoot afield.

chapter twenty-six

The Eyes Have It

Modern tournament rules allow skeet and trap shooters to start with a premounted gun, and I have a hunch that this causes many hunters to shy away from those otherwise fine shotgun games. For hunters know that live birds will catch them with their guns down, and they must then mount under pressure. Like a basketball player with but one second left to win the game, a hunter must shoot—now!

Despite all the apparent speed that certain hunting situations seem to demand, however, the mounting move should be done smoothly, confidently, and accurately if it is to be done with an expectation of consistent success. Wild poke-and-hope gun handling may score upon occasion when Lady Luck smiles, but for day-after-day results the mount should be smooth, coordinated, and practiced. Indeed, the basketball player who does swish a last-second bucket is generally one who has practiced his technique.

How Not to Do It

Many hunters make a herky-jerky, two-part mount that is terribly ineffective. When the target flushes, they will (1) struggle the gun to their shoulder and only thereafter (2) begin to point out the mark and start a swing. This is wrong because mounting the gun without reference to the target denies any smooth coordination and gun momentum. It makes the mount a separate move, whereas ideally the mounting motion will already be generating swing speed to and through the target while the gun is coming up.

The hunter who shoulders his gun first before starting to swing is letting the bird or cottontail get well ahead. He's wasting yards of distance and milliseconds of time. The hunter who does it properly, though, can shave those yards and split seconds.

A Coordinated Technique

The best mounting technique involves hand-eye coordination. It finds the hunter focusing his eyes sharply on the target immediately and keeping them there throughout the entire action sequence of mount, swing, fire, and follow-through. A shotgunner's hands will work accurately to his eyes just as a basketball player's hands will guide the ball over the lip of the rim when he concentrates his focus there. The technique goes like this:

Mounting

When the target is seen, focus your eyes on its leading edge and keep them there, zooming with the target by using your eye muscles to compensate for changes in distance and direction.

Using the leading hand as a pointer, push the gun smoothly in the direction of the moving target as you bring it up. The trigger hand

must coordinate with the leading hand's point-push dynamic as it helps to elevate the stock; hence, a swing is already building up as the gun mounts. In connection with this, the shooter should also be pivoting his body about its spinal axis to help establish the gun-body flow. Do not push outward spastically or explosively; keep it smooth and let the speed build as the swing catches the mark rather than coming out of your boots in a lunge.

As you push the gun forward, the stock will automatically clear your armpit. But do not bring the gun directly to your shoulder and then put your head down on the comb. Instead, bring the comb up to your cheekbone directly under your eye. Again, the eye is the rear sight in shotgunning, and getting it positioned squarely above the comb looking right over the barrel is a prerequisite for pointing accuracy. When the comb is touching directly under your eye, roll your shoulder forward slightly to finish the mount. One problem of the two-part mount mentioned above is that the hunter brings his head down mainly after the piece has been firmly shouldered, which may or may not mean that the eye is in the correct place. Thus proper mounting means that you bring the gun to your face, not vice versa, since the most vital part is getting the onside eye firmly in place.

Dry-firing Practice

Hunters, like basketball players, cannot hope to make perfect, split-second moves efficiently without practice. Those who don't touch a gun between seasons score by luck, not skill, as skill is acquired by doing.

Gun mounting can be practiced without ammunition expenses. Make sure the gun is empty, then practice mounting to your eye while you focus on something like a light bulb or wall ornament. Concentrate on smoothness, not sheer speed, and then discipline yourself to use the same technique afield instead of getting panicky and throwing a herky-jerky, poke-and-hope shot when the covey bursts or the partridge thunders.

Peripheral Vision and Long Leads

We've all heard that a shotgunner should focus his eyes sharply on the target's leading edge and keep them there throughout the swing, shot, and follow-through. The reason for this concentrated focus, of course, is because wingshooting is based on hand-eye coordination, and the eyes must be held on the point of intended impact if the hands are to direct the gun accurately. But there are a lot of hunters who wonder how they can make those long forward allowances on high geese and mallards if they're supposed to remain focused on the bird's bill rather than coming back to find the gun's bead or rib.

The answer lies in learning to use the two fields of normal vision, which are (1) the center focusing mechanism and (2) peripheral vision. The centering mechanism is that sharply seen area on which you use muscle power to focus. Peripheral vision is everything outside the main central spot.

Peripheral vision is important to long-range shotgunning because that's the area into which the swinging gun's muzzle works when lengthy forward allowances are generated. In other words, a hunter must expect the gun to leave his field of sharpest focus.

So how does he relate his gun's position to the bird? By being aware of the gun in peripheral vision without shifting his focus back

When you focus correctly on a bird, you should see your gun barrel—
and everything but the target—only as a blur.

to the gun. The key word is "aware." It's the tricky part of this technique, because a hunter must perform a pair of functions from the same "picture"—namely, remaining sharply focused on the target while being cognizant of the gun as a fuzzy blur.

Some dry handling will acquaint you with the awareness method. Take your gun, always making sure that it's empty, and select a focusing point such as a light bulb or small wall ornament. Focus your eyes on the object as you mount and swing the gun through it as if to set off a lead without shifting your eyes. Let the gun swing into peripheral vision. Discipline yourself to remain focused on the object, while also becoming aware of the gun's location.

Practice teaches one to feel confident without having to see the gun clearly. It may take time for a hunter to gear his mind and responses to this dual application of visual information, but it's necessary if one wishes to hit consistently by skill rather than occasionally by luck.

chapter twenty-eight

The Trigger Hand's Role in Shotgunning

Through the seasons, I've watched any number of hunters launch three-shot salvos and, upon lowering their guns, a quizzical look on their faces, protest the empty results by claiming, "But I was leading that bird!"

And I'm sure they did see a daylight gap between the muzzle and the bird.

But there is another equally important element in wingshooting besides forward allowance—pointing accuracy. A hunter may calculate the lead perfectly. However, if his gun isn't on the line of flight, he'll miss as surely as if he had shot directly at the bird's tail!

The essence of shotgun accuracy is getting one's head down snugly on the comb so that the onside eye is looking squarely over the gun. As I've written before, the eye serves as the rear sight of a shotgun while the comb acts like a sight mount. It isn't aiming per se, but it certainly does establish an alignment of eye, bore, and target.

The question is, how can we mount the gun to establish this alignment consistently? My answer: By putting more emphasis on the trigger hand's role than most books teach and most instructors preach. They commonly say that the back hand should coordinate with the leading hand in elevating the gun and then pull the trigger in time with the swing, but that's as far as it goes. Thus my advice puts greater responsibility on the trigger hand by requiring it to tuck the comb well into the cheek and under the eye. This extra effort by the back hand should help improve alignment, since it isn't uncommon to find shooters with untrained trigger hands leaving the gun well out on the rounded shoulder, which causes the hunter to stretch his neck to gain eye-to-comb contact.

To get the stock placed properly under his eye, a shooter must use firm and positive hand action. This function is often neglected in discussions of wingshooting technique, as I noted above, which may help explain why many shotgunners aren't aware of the problem.

Getting a shotgun stock under the eye consistently and holding it there through the dynamics of a swing requires more attention, however. This isn't accomplished by hand-eye coordination the way the shooter points with his leading hand, as it's not a pointing procedure. It's a mounting action, and it's learned by conscious practice. Eventually, the trigger hand may tuck the stock into place by "muscle memory," although that requires lots of work. (In fact, it isn't muscle memory that grooves a shotgunning move. Muscles don't have the capability to remember anything. It's the neurological system that grooves any physical act, via practice.)

The hunter's trigger hand must therefore be taught to tuck the gun snugly into the cheek and cheekbone so that the eye finds its centered location on the comb. Thereafter, the hand must continue to hold the gun there while the head remains down on the comb. (Clay shooters call this "putting wood to wood.") If the eye isn't kept centered, either because of an improperly mounted stock or because of head lifting, the seemingly minor misalignment at the comb will magnify downrange for a sizable pointing error.

The crux of shotgun alignment depends heavily on the trigger hand's performance in elevating and tucking away the comb. The hunter's leading hand may be tracking the target, but if his trigger hand is lazy or imprecise, it's still for naught. The importance of eye placement is best illustrated in American-style skeet and trap, both of which allow premounted guns. The scores run exceedingly high because shooters can get their eye in place atop the comb before calling their targets. If these shooters had to start with lowered guns,

The trigger hand plays an active and important role in wingshooting, tucking the gun snugly into the cheek so that the eye is properly centered on the comb.

however (as skeet originally required), the scores would average considerably lower. International-style (ISU) skeet, which mandates a low-gun start, has very, very few scores of 100 for 100.

For improved shotgun-pointing accuracy, then, spend some time assessing and practicing your trigger hand's role in mounting a shotgun to the eye. Force it to bring the comb deeply into your cheek and squarely under your eye. If this can't be done efficiently and comfortably, there's probably something wrong with your stock fit. The move should flow so that your point will place the pattern accurately on the line of flight.

Indeed, there's more for your back hand to do than just pull the trigger.

Learning to Score at Severe Angles

The overhead shot is very common in American waterfowling and dove hunting. It is also experienced more often in sporting clays as stateside layouts add high towers to their courses. And it is frequently missed, as witnessed by the many three-shot salvos launched at overhead wedges of geese and lofty, speeding mallards that come right over the blind.

One reason why we Americans have poor averages on the overhead shot is that we've normally been trained on horizontal crossers. We can swing and hit when our shotgun pivot is made around our spinal axis, but the physical movement is entirely different when we're swinging vertically. Now we're bringing our shoulders backwards, whereupon we meet the resistance of our spine. This can cause some difficulty in retaining balance while flowing into a positive follow-through.

The British are much more adept at overhead shooting than we are because they emphasize practice on driven game. The high, incoming pheasant is a classic shot in the United Kingdom, and much thought has been given by the Brits to refined techniques for this shot.

One overhead technique has received notoriety in Robert Churchill's book, *Game Shooting*. Churchill advocated a weight shift on the overhead move. It begins with the hunter's weight equally

distributed at the start, but there is a decided shift onto the rear foot (right foot of a right-handed shooter, left foot for a southpaw) as the target nears. To emphasize this shift, the hunter's leading foot can exert some toe pressure to ease his body backward. For optimal results, the weight shift should be done with rhythm and timing to coordinate with the target's line and velocity. Moreover, the shift helps to extend the body's action for a definite follow-through.

The second technique was described by Percy Stanbury in *Shotgun Marksmanship*. Stanbury, one of England's great coaches and a former champion competitor, taught shooters to put their weight on the leading foot and keep it there throughout the swing, lead, and follow-through. This keeps your feet solidly anchored for balance and forces you to make the upward and overhead move by arching your spine.

Both Churchill and Stanbury tended to advise their students to take the target directly overhead, when it is the closest and requires the least forward allowance.

Which is better, Churchill or Stanbury? I like Stanbury's idea best when standing in water or a snug blind, as it keeps my weight centered. The Churchill method, on the other hand, works best when your feet are on a solid base and you have some room to make the rearward weight shift. Regardless of which technique you choose, remember that these are both athletic moves that can improve with practice.

The type of forward allowance system one uses is also a factor. Typically, hunters apply the sustained lead, in which the gun comes up a calculated distance ahead of the target, tracks the mark a short way, and is fired with the muzzle out front. Unfortunately, however, there is a marked tendency for shooters to slow their swing as the moment of truth arrives. Many hunters stop at trigger pull. To score with the sustained lead, the gun's speed must jibe with the target's velocity and line.

For enhanced gun dynamics, a hunter might well use the swing-through or pull-ahead system, since both necessitate an acceleration of the gun.

In the swing-through system, the gun starts behind the target and is swung aggressively through it. The shot is fired as the muzzle

chapter twenty-nine

The overhead shot is frequently missed by shooters trained on
horizontal crossers because it calls for an entirely different technique.

begins to pass the target's leading edge. An important note is that distance plays a role in the trigger pull: The higher and faster a bird is, the longer one should delay the pull to let forward allowance build.

Not all hunters like the dynamics of the swing-through. They lack gun speed and timing, or they don't feel comfortable swinging from behind the target. For them, the pull-ahead system is preferred. This movement begins with the muzzle mounted directly on the bird. The muzzle is then swung ahead smoothly to open daylight, and the shot is fired while the gun continues in an extended swing and follow-through.

Whether it's waterfowl, doves, or sporting clays, put some athleticism into your technique for a smooth overhead swing that also allows for a full, vertical follow-through.

Hitting Long-Range Flushing Shots

Mallards that vault close in from a beaver pond as you break through the alder rim, quail that burst from directly under a pointer's nose, and tight-sitting pheasants and sharptails that flush from underfoot—all are easy, short-range shots that give the hunter a cushion of time. But interestingly enough, their proximity to the gun also gives an impression of speed, causing many hunters to react quickly and shoot with a fast swing.

Let woodies spring from the slough at 35 yards, however, or let wind-spooky sharptails flush at the fringe of scattergun range, and many hunters will react differently: They'll move deliberately, as if aiming the shot rather than pointing and swinging it. I've done it myself, have watched it happen dozens of times to others, and have had readers' letters asking why they can hit a fast crosser at 20 yards but invariably miss a climber at 35 yards or thereabouts.

The answer is that there's an optical illusion involved in long-range flushes. Distant objects appear to be moving slower than those close up, even if they have the same speed. The pheasant threshing out at 5 yards is a flurry of action, and it excites a hunter. But the same pheasant at 35 yards looks slower and gives one the impression of having plenty of time to go through the move-mount-shoot sequence, whereas in fact the opposite is true. The close-in flush,

©CHRIS DORSEY

Birds in the distance only look slow—swing briskly and follow through!

however dramatic, can be handled easier because the bird will be in range longer. It is the distant bird that needs to be taken now.

Let me give you another example of this optical illusion. When you're in the airport, jets coming in for a landing seem to settle on cupped wings like a majestic Canada goose. They appear to be floating in at terribly slow speed. The fact is, they're landing at more than a hundred miles per hour. Thus distance fools a hunter into believing that his long-range flushes are slow, which in turn prompts him to be too deliberate. The far flush is out of effective pattern range before the shot string gets there.

The optical illusion also causes us to calculate forward allowances on the short side. But it can take a load of high-velocity lead 6s or steel 2s about one-eighth of a second to cross 40 yards of upland cover or marshland, and in that time an accelerating bird can fly anywhere from three to eight feet, depending on the angles. It is totally wrong, then, to "draw a bead" on such apparently pedestrian birds. Not only are the birds as fast as close-in flushes, but the shot charge must fight more air resistance in going from muzzle to mark.

How do we hit the long-range flushers? The first step is understanding and overcoming the impact of the optical illusion. The bird may look slow, but it's beginning to carry progressively more air speed. The second step is reacting quickly and smoothly. Pausing a second to size up the situation is tantamount to disaster. A pause is okay when the bird flushes close in, because you have 40 yards of effective range remaining. But a flush at 30 to 35 yards leaves you with just 10 to 20 yards of pattern density. Consequently, there's no time to dawdle, to second-guess yourself, or to "bead up" and take deliberate aim. Let the move-mount-shoot sequence begin *muy pronto*.

High Birds

As I wrote in the last section, when you stand on an airport observation deck and watch giant jetliners land, you'd swear they floated in like feathers. They seem to hang above the end of the runway, flaps down and barely moving, like a mallard about to drop into the decoys. But when you stand at the end of the runway as one of those streamlined jets whistles in, it's a different picture. Close up, those babies really move!

What does all this have to do with wingshooting? Plenty. For like a distant airliner, a lofty duck or goose looks a lot slower than it actually is. It's an optical illusion of sorts, one that causes more than a few hunters (including me) to miss. We think that the high bird is going so slowly that we can be rather casual about our swing, practically aiming just ahead of the bird as we track along. And everything looks so good over the gun's rib or bead that when we pull the trigger we honestly expect the bird to buckle and come straight down.

But it normally doesn't happen that way. Nor does it happen on the next shot. Or the next. The bird keeps flying with not a feather ruffled. Hey, what's wrong with these shells?

Chances are there's nothing wrong with the loads, of course. The fault lies with gun speed. Because the bird looked slow, we swung deliberately. And as a result of our pedestrian stroke, there was never

chapter thirty-one

©BILL BUCKLEY

any coordination between the bird's de facto speed and our swing speed. We simply shot a mile behind a truly fast target by taking our good ol' time in swinging the gun. In fact, there are times when our movement isn't much of a swing at all but rather a draggy aim ahead of the target.

The point is, a shotgun must be swung briskly whether the bird is barely 20 yards away over the decoys or 50 yards up and looking like it's loafing along. It's a good bet that "tall" bird is going virtually as fast as the one that buzzes the blocks and looks like a lowhouse skeet clay. Indeed, the high bird might be going faster because it can get a shove from the wind.

As hunters, we must scrupulously avoid taking unreachable shots. Nothing is more frustrating than sharing a marsh with skybusters. But all high shooting is not skybusting. To score consistently on those reachable long-range birds, meaning those at 35 yards or more, a hunter must first overcome the tendency to be deliberate in his point and swing. His mind must be programmed to jibe with the bird's actual speed, not its apparent speed. Once confident with that, the hunter can put some athletic grace and speed into his technique to swing boldly and generate the long forward allowances necessary.

One mistake made by many hunters is to start ahead of the apparently slow bird and, with a laggardly move, try to measure off what they believe to be the best lead. This is generally called the "sustained lead." Its weakness is that there's a tendency to aim, and to stop at trigger pull. What's needed is a more dynamic technique, one that builds momentum into the gun itself to help pull the hunter smoothly, briskly, and positively along in coordination with the target's actual speed.

This technique is something I've come to term the "extended fast swing." It begins with the gun coming up behind the bird so that the hunter must overcome gun inertia to catch the target and pass it. But unlike the basic fast swing (also called the swing-through method), the trigger isn't pulled as the muzzle blur passes the bird. Trigger pull is delayed until a sizeable amount of daylight appears between bird and muzzle. The exact amount of daylight will depend on personal and physical factors, such as swing speed and the target's range. It may take a while for each individual to learn exactly how he or she is timed for this technique. By racing ahead of the bird before firing, the hunter should be increasing his or her swing speed and building gun energy for a positive follow-through. Those are the ingredients so often lacking in the common practice of starting out front and aiming to a point in space without coordinating with the target's actual speed. As a rule of thumb, you're going to start scoring when you think you've gotten much too far ahead because high targets demand extremely long leads that can be difficult to visualize.

What are we talking about in terms of calculated leads? A mallard nearing 50 yards, which is in range of a tight pattern of steel BBs, will require a forward allowance of 10 to 15 feet, depending upon the true range and the bird's speed. But you can't measure off those 10 to 15 feet with a draggy gun. Those leads must be slapped on by a dynamic fowling piece that races ahead of the mark aggressively and launches its shot string without slowing or stopping at trigger pull. To aim 12 feet in front of an overhead goose like a rifleman holding on a bull's-eye is a sure miss.

chapter thirty-two

The Trouble with
Sustained Lead Is . . .

American wingshooting literature tells us that stateside scribes have traditionally ballyhooed two methods of generating forward allowance while shooting—the sustained-lead and the swing-through method. Invariably, you'll read that the sustained-lead is best suited to long-range shooting, while the swing-through method should be applied mainly to close shots of 30 to 35 yards or less. Consequently, the majority of waterfowlers and dove hunters have long accepted sustained lead as their modus operandi.

And they've missed, sometimes repeatedly and embarrassingly so.

Why should anyone ever miss using a technique that is so simple that all a hunter must do is calculate the lead, bring his gun up ahead of the target by that calculated amount, and pull the trigger while sustaining forward allowance? There are millions of reasons. From where I've stood behind both clay and game shooters, however, the main reason for missing with sustained lead is failure to maintain a smooth swing as you pull the trigger. Slowing or stopping the gun while pulling the trigger is tantamount to disaster when the target is moving at 40 to 60 miles per hour.

Many shooters will question whether a bird or clay can fly far enough during the time between their mental command to fire and the actual muzzle report to cause a total miss, but that is in fact the case.

©CHRIS DORSEY

He who hesitates is lost. Even in sustained-lead shooting, the gun must be in constant motion.

An overhead or crossing target going just 40 mph moves at the rate of 720 inches per second, which converts to 60 feet, or about the distance between the pitching rubber and home plate on a big league baseball diamond. Now if the gun is slowed and stopped for just one-tenth of that second, the target covers about 72 inches, or six feet—far more than an effective pattern can cover. If you were leading the target by five feet when you began to slow while pulling the trigger, you would have lost most of your forward allowance.

Why would anyone slow his swing with the sustained-lead method? One reason is that shooters wrongly try to be precise with their pattern placement. They shoot more like riflemen than shotgunners. They'll take their eyes off the target and aim with the rib or beads, and they'll concentrate on pulling the trigger while allowing their swing to die.

Another reason is caused by an optical illusion that makes a long-range target seem slower than it actually is. A target crossing at 45 yards appears slower than one of the same velocity at just 15 yards; hence, a hunter is easily lulled into making an equally slow mount and swing, which doesn't have enough of its own energy and gun-generated momentum to track with the target.

How can a hunter overcome these weaknesses in the sustained-lead method? This can be accomplished by selecting the right shotgun and learning self-discipline. The shotgun should have sufficient length and weight, and a slightly barrel-heavy condition isn't all bad. The old-timers liked Long Toms because they provided momentum for a smooth, sustained swing, thereby helping the shooter overcome his natural tendency to slow and stop while pulling the trigger. Consequently, I prefer barrels of 28 to 30 inches on repeaters and 30- to 32-inch barrels on doubles.

In regard to self-discipline, a hunter must visualize the forward allowance and fire without glancing back to the gun to aim. The focal point must always be the target, and the technique must be based on hand-eye coordination rather than riflelike aiming.

Finally, a hunter must force himself to maintain gun speed through the trigger pull and a positive follow-through. Anything less is just another miss.

The trouble with sustained lead, then, is that it is simple in concept but complex in its application, especially during the final phase when gun speed, trigger pull, and follow-through must come together perfectly.

chapter thirty-three

How Nash Buckingham Did It

Nash Buckingham was one of the most popular outdoor writers in the early half of our twentieth century. Reprints of his books sell briskly, and the first editions carry collectors' prices.

A superb athlete in his college years, Buckingham was reputed to have converted that natural coordination into equally superb long-range duck shooting. His pet guns were a pair of A. H. Fox doubles refined by a barrelsmith named Burt Becker, who overbored the guns and chambered them for the then-new 3-inch 12-gauge magnum. His load was $1^3/_8$ ounces of copper-plated 4s. While Buckingham's guns were custom made, the same basic concept was available as the HE Grade Fox, also known as the Super-Fox.

But just having a Burt Becker double or a Super-Fox doesn't make one a wizard at long-range wingshooting. There must be a swing system to generate the necessary forward allowance. And in Buckingham's case, not only was there a system, but it was a rather different one. For lack of a better term, we'll call it the "moving spot" system.

Shotgun coaches today teach shooters to keep their eyes focused sharply on the target while the gun rides in peripheral vision. But Nash Buckingham reversed that. He explained his method in an article titled "Are We Shooting 8-Gauge Guns?" in the 1960 *Gun*

Digest by stating that the target should be "carried in your subconscious vision" as you pick out the right lead and concentrate on that spot ahead of the target. In other words, Buckingham focused on the point of interception, not the bird. But he perforce closes with the cautionary remark that "you can't intercept it [the bird] by firing at a fixed spot ahead—your gun must hit a moving spot."

In essence, the Buckingham "moving spot" system has these four main steps: (1) observe the target's flight line, (2) calculate the forward allowance, (3) focus on the point of interception as the gun is being aligned and swung in a sustained lead, and (4) fire and flow into a follow-through as the eyes continue to track that moving spot while the trailing target is tucked into your subconscious vision (or, perhaps, peripheral vision).

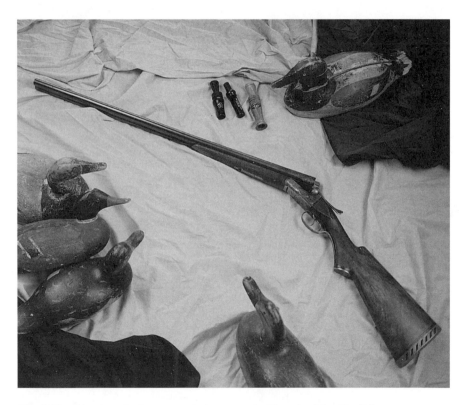

Nash Buckingham's famous custom-made Fox double, Bo-Whoop, refined by barrelsmith Burt Becker, who overbored the barrels and chambered them for 3-inch 12-guage magnum loads.

The Buckingham system, then, is our normal sustained-lead method with a reversal in the optical practice. He focused over the gun barrels at the lead, terming it the "moving spot," while we look at the target.

I rather like Nash's concept. It forces the shooter to get his eyes up front. Moreover, some people have difficulty maintaining alignment and swing speed when the visual gap between target and muzzle begins to stretch out 10 to 20 feet or more.

I've tried the system on high doves, ducks, and sporting clays, and it works perfectly when the target's line is visualized and maintained. But as Buckingham wrote, it is a moving spot, not a stationary bull's-eye. So keep your head down and follow through!

How Far Is It?
Tips for Improving
Your Range-Judging Skills

Several years ago I happened to bag my limit early and stopped along the perimeter of a waterfowl refuge famous for its regular contingent of skybusters. I had a range finder with me, so I pushed into the cattail growth among the shooters where I could measure the height of the geese as they crossed the refuge boundary into the field of fire.

I discovered that it wasn't unusual for the shooters to trigger three-shot salvoes at geese 80 to 90 yards away, and assorted barrages greeted more than a few flocks that were a full 100 yards high. What made matters worse, I learned, was that some of the skybusters were also using the most notorious goose-crippling load, steel No. 4s.

There are two good reasons why waterfowlers should refine their range-judging skills. The first is to prevent the crippling of birds flying beyond the effective patterning and penetrating range of a shotgun and load. The second is to be able to select shots at optimal killing ranges, thus maximizing shooting opportunities.

How does a waterfowler improve his range-judging abilities? The easiest way is to carry a range-finding device while in the field. Waterfowlers can choose from a variety of range finders, which vary considerably in design and price but come in two basic types: laser and coincidence models. Laser range finders can be expensive—often costing more than your pet pumpgun—while coincidence devices are quite affordable. Range finders developed for bowhunters can be used by shotgunners as well, since target ranges in both sports are comparable.

Without a range finder, hunters must learn how to visually determine distance. A neighborhood baseball diamond is a good place to learn to judge distances encountered by shotgunners. For example, there is a distance of 20 yards from the pitcher's mound to home plate, 30 yards between bases, and roughly 40 yards from home plate to second base. A football, which is roughly the same size as a mallard, is a good object with which to judge distances. To visualize a passing mallard at 40 yards, place the football on second base and take a hard look at it from home plate.

A football gridiron, where 5- and 10-yard increments are clearly marked, is another good place to practice judging distance. A good exercise is to stand on a goal line while a hunting partner holds a football aloft and walks slowly backwards from 20 to 60 yards away. Have your partner toss the football in the air and note how small it appears at maximum shooting ranges. This can be a humbling experience for those who believe they routinely kill birds beyond 60 yards.

Is it farther than second base? Visualizing distances can help you become a better wingshot.

©BILL BUCKLEY

Birds above the treetops may be closer than you think.

Thus far I've discussed methods of judging distance at ground level, using a horizontal background to assist in determining range. However, it is much more difficult to judge the distance of targets against the sky, where no frame of reference is available. As noted by Sir Ralph Payne-Gallwey in his classic tome, *High Pheasants in Theory and Practice*, "An overhead object appears much smaller than one at the same distance on the ground."

So how do we learn to judge objects passing overhead without a range-finding device? This skill can be honed in the city by observing the height of buildings. In my area, there is a bank that stands about 38 yards high, which is well within the working range of a modified-choked 12-bore. When I ask fellow hunters if they would shoot at pigeons flitting about the roof of the building, they regularly view them as out of range or requiring a magnum 10-gauge.

Outside my window is a big pine tree, and when a mourning dove arrows over it, my perception is that the bird is flying at extreme shotgun range. My range finder, however, says it's only 35 yards from my desk to the top of the pine. Thus hunters must take into account this optical illusion when shooting at targets passing against the sky.

Exploding Skeet Shooting Myths

S keet shooting started around the time of World War I, when a group of New England bird hunters decided that they needed a way to practice the myriad angles encountered afield. Charles E. Davis, a businessman from Andover, Massachusetts, is normally given credit for originating the idea. Another of the primary contributors was his neighbor William H. Foster, who soon became the editor of the now defunct *National Sportmen* and *Hunting and Fishing* magazines.

Skeet is a Scandinavian word meaning "to shoot." And shoot they did. Thanks primarily to hunters, skeet fields flourished throughout the United States. The original rules of skeet favored field gunning. They required a shooter to keep his gun in a lowered position until the target appeared, and the targets were not released instantly. Instead, they were launched within three seconds after the shooter called "Pull!" Thus the shooter did not know precisely when the target would pop out of the skeet houses, and once it did he had to go through the point, mount, and swing sequence with the target already airborne. If that isn't close to the demands of field-style shotgun handling, what is?

But, alas, skeet has suffered tragically from negative publicity in the post–World War II era. It is not unusual to hear someone (often someone who has never shot skeet) criticize skeet as a perfectionist's game, a "groove shooter's" sport that has nothing to do with hunting. Some of this criticism stems from changes in tournament rules during the 1950s. It was only then that modern skeet rules dropped the low-gun requirement to allow shooters to solidly pre-mount their gun before calling for the clay. Moreover, liberalized rules also mandated an instantly released target, which meant that modern skeet no longer requires a shooter to watch for a variably timed target released with a lowered gun. I'll readily agree that modern tournament skeet has little in common with field-style shotgunning.

But here's the rub: Hunters who are solely interested in practicing for the field need not follow tournament rules. Nothing in the world says one must pre-mount the gun in practice skeet. You can step on that skeet station and stand with a lowered gun just as they did in the days of Charles Davis and William Foster. Likewise, you don't have to shoot instantly released targets in skeet practice; merely ask the trap boy to give you the variably timed pulls, and you're in business like those who originated skeet as a bird hunter's game. Indeed, tournament skeet and practice skeet are two different worlds, and most gun clubs are open for far more practice than they ever are for competitions.

Another knock on skeet is that its range is too limited and therefore does not simulate real hunting. Let's face it: no clay-target game will ever simulate live game perfectly, not even sporting clays. But the main point is that skeet does give a shotgunner his chance to take all sorts of angles, from overhead outgoers to right-angle crossers both right and left to a straightaway and an overhead snap shot. Some skeet clays are high; some are low. And they all must be pointed at and swung on if you are to score well.

That, my friends, is the crux of practice skeet using the original low-gun, variably timed release. It gives one practice in gun-handling technique. The actual range to the target makes little difference. The point, pivot, swing, and follow-through that score at 20- to 25-yard skeet distances are also the same physical moves necessary for 40- to 50-yard shots. The longer ranges become easier to handle when a shotgunner has become comfortable with the coordination, tempo, and rhythm required for the same angles, albeit a bit closer. If you can carry the technique learned on a skeet field into the blind or uplands, you will not only score better but will make a higher percentage of centered hits for clean kills and positive retrieves.

Confidence is a big factor in successful shotgunning, and skeet can help you generate that confidence by keeping you familiar with your bird guns. So ignore the popular myths about skeet and approach it the way it was meant to be used—as a gun game for the game gun.

chapter thirty-six

The Essence of Sporting Clays

American sportsmen have spent decades talking about clay target games that simulate field shooting, but until recently nothing of that sort had come along to capture the public's fancy. True, there were Quail Walks and Grouse Walks when some enterprising clubs placed trap machines along a fencerow or a trail through a woodlot. And there was also a game called Crazy Quail, which consisted of a single trap machine placed in a pit and swiveled to throw targets through a full 360-degree circle. But all of these were merely flashes in the proverbial pan. They gained no widespread acceptance.

In recent years, however, a pair of clay-target games have come out of Great Britain and Europe to change all that. The games are known generically as sporting clays. They can be as tough as a woody whipping through tree crowns, as demanding as a high mallard, as spirited as a springing teal, as humorous as a cottontail cutting through the bramble, as changeable as the wind across a broad marsh, and as rewarding as a double on ruffed grouse. And they have indeed caught on with hunters who have tried them. But although sporting clays has gained some publicity and followers in the U.S. and Canada, sportsmen on this side of the Atlantic Ocean still have something to learn about these games.

The first thing is that there are two different forms of sporting clays. One of these is British sporting clays, which is the form practiced most widely stateside. Its format is predicated on doubles at all stands; seldom does British sporting clays use just a single. To spice up British clays, however, three types of doubles have evolved: simultaneous doubles, in which both targets are launched at the same time; trailing pairs, in which the targets are thrown singly but as rapidly as the trapper can recock and reload the machine, meaning a double flying virtually single file; and report doubles, in which the second target is thrown on the sound of the shooter's first shot. Simultaneous and trailing pairs generally come from the same trap, while report pairs frequently come out of a pair of traps and present criss-crossing or otherwise different angles.

Get ready! The trapper can release the target at any time within three seconds after you call "Pull!"

The second form of sporting clays is commonly known as FITASC (pronounced "Fit-ask"). This is the international form of sporting clays, and its initials stand for the organization's name: Fédération International de Tir aux Armes Sportives de Chasse. Unlike British sporting clays, which finds the shooter getting three to five pairs of the same targets at each stand, FITASC mixes up the angles and target sizes while also employing a considerable number of singles. The goal of FITASC is to make every shot different rather than repeat chances. Moreover, FITASC rules permit two shots at singles, all of which brings it closer to what field shooting is all about. Unfortunately, FITASC has not yet been firmly established stateside, but when it does finally gain a foothold it, not British clays, will be called the hunter's game. Gun clubs that now throw sporting clays would do well to look into the rules and concepts of FITASC.

Whether a layout's course follows the format of British clays or FITASC, however, it's a fun time and learning experience. It can also be a humbling experience for hunters who have a bit of an ego problem. Sporting clays in any form tests the shooter's skill. The targets can range from slow, settling-in shots, through "rabbit" targets bouncing merrily along at just 10 yards, and rising scorchers at 25 yards, to high passing and overhead chances 40 to 50 yards up. By the time a beginner finishes his first round of sporting clays, he may feel that he has twisted his gun's barrel into a pretzel by trying to hit targets that slant into a gully, followed by targets that climb steeply from an orchard, followed by clays that bound along a grassy field, followed by saucers which angle in, angle out, rise to the left, flare to the right, come from behind, and spin through a small opening in the crowns of tall trees. The important point is to approach these initial rounds of sporting clays with a proper, relaxed frame of mind. It is shotgunning in its most demanding sense, and everyone has a lot to learn. Everyone.

The rules of American sporting clays and FITASC require a low-gun starting position. The top of the stock must be held below armpit level until the target is seen. Too, the trapper can release the target(s) at any time within a three-second period after the shooter has called "Pull!" or "Ready!" Both of these rules bring the game closer to reality for a sportsman who's primarily a field shot.

Both versions of sporting clays have rules which require that targets be presented to simulate actual game shooting conditions. The current FITASC rules state that "a sporting layout must be equipped with a sufficient number of traps so that the competitors will shoot under conditions resembling game shooting—partridges, pheasants, ducks, and rabbits; in front, low and high, in battue, crossing and quartering, on fields or in woods; the targets may be hidden or not by trees and bushes." This should gladden the hearts of bird hunters who formerly have charged that skeet and trap are "groove" games.

A number of different target sizes are used in sporting clays. The standard target is close in appearance to the American skeet and trap saucer, but it is slightly (just slightly) larger and harder. Its basic diameter is 110 millimeters, give or take 2 millimeters. Other targets are the midi (mid-sized) at 90 millimeters, and the mini (sometimes termed the super-mini by overseas shooters) at 60 millimeters, which are also shaped like the standard clay with obvious domes. Added to this list are the rabbit, which is a rock-hard target made with an ultra-thick rim to withstand the impact with the ground as it bounces along; the battue, a very thin target about the diameter of a standard clay but with a small dome and the in-flight characteristic of twisting and curling; and the "rocket," which is terribly hard and, although not super fast, difficult to break with a fringe hit.

The smaller clays are used to present optical illusions; they give the appearance of being much farther away than they are. The battue carries a lot of its original speed as it flies like a phonograph record. Its deceptive velocity and curling tendencies cause many to shoot well behind and/or lift their head in an effort to follow its flight. The rocket clay is a challenge simply because it normally takes a centered hit to break it.

Which guns and loads for sporting clays? If you're a hunter who is looking for some off-season improvement, your field guns will do just fine. A person who becomes serious about the sport and decides to give tournaments a whirl will probably want to take a hard look at specialized sporting clays pieces. But meanwhile there's absolutely nothing wrong with the ol' fowling stick. Full choke isn't ideal, but if that's what you hunt with, why not use it? I've seen a number of hunters do reasonably well with a full-choke gun, as the essence of this game is the swing, not a few extra inches of pattern width.

In general, though, improved-cylinder is a better choke for sporting clays, and a double-bored improved-cylinder and modified fits quite well. A lot of sporting clays shots can come between 20 to 30 yards, in which case the modified choke isn't at all bad.

And what about the smaller gauges? Be my guest. The 20-gauge can score well in sporting clays, especially with a 1-ounce load of No. 8s. The 28-gauge gets a little thin in the fringe for many sporting clays stands, but if you center the clay, you'll score it. The .410 bore is a tad dicey, but a 3-inch load of No. 7s can pick up a surprising number or clays when you point and swing properly. Just don't expect target-shattering performances from the .410. Indeed, a round

Great for all shooting levels, a sporting clays course is the perfect place to learn the basics of wingshooting.

of sporting clays with a .410 illustrates why so much game is crippled and lost with this peewee bore, as the hits will be light and chippy rather than overpowering.

The loads should be target loads. Rules of both basic sporting and FITASC mandate sizes from Nos. 7½ through 9. In British-style sporting clays, the shot charge is limited to 1½ ounces with a maximum powder charge of 3¼ drams equivalent (1,255 fps). For FITASC, the load can go to a full 1¼ ounces of shot.

As an all-around pellet, the No. 8 is a good selection. It seems able to break most sporting clays targets at all legitimate ranges while also giving good pattern density from an improved-cylinder choke. Some shooters like to use No. 9s on close-range clays, and that's acceptable. The No. 7½ seems at its best on the ultra-hard rocket target. Luckily, the loading industry makes available inexpensive promotion or dove loads with just 1-ounce 8s, and they will normally suffice for anyone who is working his first trip or two around a sporting clays course. If you're a handloader, use your typical skeet or trap recipe with No. 8s. As time goes on, you may want to refine your load selections and carry different shot sizes for various challenges, but don't let those things bother you at the start.

Just get started! If you love waterfowling and shotguns, you can't help but love the forms of sporting clays.

The Makings of a Sporting Clays Gun

The game of sporting clays was developed in England to simulate the flights of game birds in natural covers. A rabbit trap was then devised to roll clay targets along the ground, as hares have always been a considerable part of British and European hunting. Because of sporting clays' close relationship to field shooting, one would think that a basic hunting gun should be adequate. And it is. Sporting clays is a great way for hunters to remain familiar with their pet bird guns during the off-season.

But as always, sport shooters clamored for special models refined for a specific contest. This demand became emphatic when the game took on a competitive slant, because tournament shooters want every bit of gun efficiency they can get. Thus we now have the sporting clays models.

Essentially, a sporting clays gun combines the responsiveness of a good bird gun with the discipline of a target-grade piece. The responsiveness aspect explains itself. The gun should start easily on fast-breaking clays. That doesn't mean it should whip into action like a 5$\frac{1}{2}$-pound 28-gauge double. Which is where the term "discipline" comes in.

A disciplined shotgun is one that moves smoothly from start to the finish of a follow-through. Many lightweight bird guns don't do

Long-barreled over-unders like this one are common in the game of sporting clays—and for good reasons.

that; they spring quickly, then die in the hunter's hands because they lack frontal momentum to help pull the shooter into a positive lead and follow-through. This is one reason why hunters often score poorly on sporting clays with short-barreled and/or lightweight smallbores.

Expert sporting clays shooters have therefore gone to barrels that are considerably longer than most Americans would equate with upland hunting and, in some instances, waterfowling. Barrels of 30 and 32 inches are in vogue on both over-unders and autoloaders. Although still viable, 28-inch barrels are about the shortest any serious competitor would consider.

But always remember, as stated above, the gun's barrel length isn't the sole criterion. A muzzle-heavy hang can upset smooth, easy, uniform starts and tire one's shoulders when taking as many as 10 shots on a stand. The barrels must blend into the total gun so that responsiveness isn't sacrificed. Thus the ideal sporting clays piece has a slight weight-forward balance, but does not weigh down the individual shooter's strength and technique.

©CHRIS DORSEY

Many sporting clays courses are open year-round.

chapter thirty-eight

Barrel Length:
The Long and Short of It

It was another era, even before World War II, when my grandfather pulled a shotgun from the rack of a local hardware store and handed it to me. I buckled under that long-barreled piece and wondered what hunters saw in them. Why this fascination with heavy Long Toms?

As I came to know, the traditional justifications for such robust waterfowling guns were threefold: (1) in a carryover concept from black-powder days, they promised optimal ballistics; (2) they supposedly provided accurate pattern placement due to their lengthy sighting radii; and (3) the forward weight supplied a momentum of its own for smoothness and a positive follow-through. Many hunters also equated long, lean barrels with tight patterning, but that myth has been discredited time and again. Patterning is a matter of gun and load compatibility, not simply barrel length.

Long barrels were important in burning black powder, but my own chronographing indicates that the velocity loss between 26- and 30-inch barrels isn't significant with modern smokeless powders. For several seasons, I bagged my high mallards and geese with a 26-inch-barreled Remington SP-10 and factory steel loads, and I observed no impact differences between it and other 10s I've used with 30- and 32-inch barrels.

The momentum of a long barrel can help you follow through.

The sighting radius is a misleading one. Scatterguns aren't supposed to be used with a squinty-eyed aim by lining up beads or a rib-bead picture. A shotgunner theoretically gets his accuracy by hand-eye coordination, his eyes always focused sharply on the target's leading edge while the gun is seen only as a blur in peripheral vision. Moreover, if a hunter gets his head down properly on the comb, the barrel disappears below the receiver. Thus it makes no real difference if the barrel is 26 or 32 inches long, because one is not looking at it anyway.

The weight-forward argument has some validity. Many hunters do not have complete technique, and it's sometimes difficult to be smooth and to follow through in a cramped blind. Here the momentum of a long barrel pulls one through, whereas one might have stopped otherwise upon pulling the trigger. As a split-the-difference approach, hunters will find 28-inch barrels nicely suited to repeaters and 30-inchers tolerable on doubles with their compact action bodies.

Rather than being a slave to traditions, then, a modern waterfowler can opt for a shorter barrel than those of the long-range wonder of yore.

Guns with a Second Chance

Have you ever wondered which shotguns will deliver the fastest follow-up shots without upsetting alignment? By this I don't mean just rattling off two or three shots for the sake of making noise on the marsh—I mean snapping them off posthaste with the full potential of hitting something. Anybody can just blast away.

In both theory and practice, some shotguns provide firepower with more impact on the shooter's shoulder so that the gun's muzzle jumps above a target's line of flight. Invariably it knocks itself out of alignment with the shooter's eye. And in a situation where so much depends upon hand-eye coordination, anything that upsets natural alignment is tantamount to disaster.

The shooter must then fight to recover from the recoil dynamic so that his head will again find the sweet spot on the comb for renewed alignment. As I mentioned in an earlier chapter, one's eye serves as the rear sight in shotgunning. If it isn't squarely behind the receiver looking parallel with the bore axis, it causes the same basic inaccuracies that occur when a rifle's rear sight is out of adjustment. Thus the speed with which a shotgun's action gets back into battery for a second or third shot is virtually insignificant unless the shooter can also recover quickly enough from recoil to utilize the mechanism's quickness. The theoretical ideal is reached with single-trigger over-unders when the lower barrel is fired first, and in low-recoil (generally gas-operated) autoloaders.

Experts have long considered the single-trigger over-under to be the fastest second shot in wing-gunning, and one look at the winningest guns in skeet, sporting clays, and trap doublers bolsters their point: When tournament competitors need two shots fast, they rely on the stackbarrel.

What gives the over-under its basis for swift second shots? Mainly, the fact that the lower barrel's depressed location places that bore's axis below the comb line to create what is known as "straight-line" recoil. This brings the piece backward into the shooter's shoulder hollow rather than encouraging it to jump upward. The result is an easier, quicker recovery. And since the single trigger is ready to go on an over-under as soon as the rebound dissipates, a shooter can regain his alignment and let added, accurately pointed patterns fly immediately. There is, however, one negative to the over-under's performance. Heavy loads that overpower the gun can sometimes cancel out the niceties of straight-line recoil.

Remember, only the lower tube of an over-under offers this straight-line recoil dynamic. The upper barrel's bore axis almost always runs above the comb line, and from this high-sitting position it gains a leverage on the gun that translates into considerably more noticeable recoil, with a definite muzzle-jump characteristic. This is why the over-under's lower barrel is normally set to be fired first: Its recoil is easier to manage than the top barrel's.

Although most persnickety shotgun scribes have focused on the over-under as the smoothbore with the fastest second shot, I must interject that I am slowly being won over by the low-recoil autoloaders. There may be faster actions than those found on the gas-operated autoloaders, but I'm not certain that a hunter can take advantage of the greater speed. I've never had to stand around waiting for a Remington 1100 or 11-87, or a Beretta A-303, to close; they've always been back in battery by the time my finger closed down on the trigger. Moreover, gas systems drag out the recoil sensation, lessening the peak impulses and thus reducing gun jump for an easier, quicker recovery. My own feeling has long been that if somebody can design a low-recoil autoloader that has the handling qualities and responsiveness of a fine double, they'll have the best of both worlds.

Anyone who has followed me this far has begun to understand that a shotgun's muzzle climb is about the biggest bugaboo in fast follow-up shooting. If the barrel would just "hang" in place, we could absorb the backward thrust of recoil and get back into alignment immediately. It's forcing the barrel back down that takes time and prompts mistakes.

Winchester Supreme Field Over-Under

In recent years, we've learned how to tame muzzle jump. It's called "porting," which is nothing more than placing various-sized holes in the top of the barrel out near the muzzle. Most porting is done just before the choke taper begins, and its purpose is to create an action-reaction situation that puts a downward (reaction) force on the barrel to help hold it in place. Thus we can attach a corollary to the above list of ideally suited shotguns for the fast, accurately aligned shots. Not only will the single-trigger over-unders and gas-operated autoloaders be optimal theoretical selections, but even they will be enhanced by the inclusion of ported barrels.

©BILL BUCKLEY

tips and tidbits

Taming Shotgun Recoil

The heavy, high-velocity loads of waterfowling make robust recoil an integral part of the sport. Firing this ammunition can inflict intense pain on shooters and often results in missed follow-up shots. In some cases, repeated exposure to punishing recoil causes shooters to develop a flinch.

Many waterfowlers seek a solution to abusive recoil by modifying their shotguns. Since the start of recoil takes place in the bore, running from chamber to muzzle, it takes some skullduggery to mitigate it. The first step is to obtain a technologically advanced recoil pad. For optimal results and comfort, recoil pads made of sorbothane are recommended. They should be fitted for length of pull appropriate to your hunting clothes. A fitted gun with the correct pitch seems to kick less.

Gun weight is another factor that has a large impact on felt recoil. The heavier the gun relative to a load's weight and velocity, the lower the sensible recoil. Placing lead shot in the butt stock's cavity and inserting a lead slug in the tubular magazine are ways to beef up light guns to offset recoil.

Barrel length also influences the recoil sustained by shooters. Although American marketing trends have tended toward increasingly shorter barrels, it is long shotgun barrels that help reduce recoil. The longer the barrel, the more volume powder gases have in which to expand, thus reducing the pressure within the barrel and, consequently, the recoil produced as these gases exit the muzzle. Longer barrels also have the added benefit of being easier on a shooter's ears.

Other ways of mitigating recoil are lengthening the forcing cone and using a back-bored barrel. Both of these alterations to the interior of a shotgun barrel expedite smoother wad flow. This effect doesn't eliminate recoil, but takes the sting out of it. Some years ago, I had a foreign double with half-inch forcing cones that kicked like the proverbial devil. I had a gunsmith ream them to a full two inches long, and the double's recoil characteristics changed abruptly to a more comfortable level.

Trapshooters have long been innovators in the campaign against recoil. Many use compressible stock mechanisms and butt inserts

Reducing recoil can help you stay on target for follow-up shots, and recover quickly for shots at other birds.

known as reducers. They also have promoted the practice of barrel porting, another gun modification that can reduce gun jump and recoil. Ports allow gases to spurt upward, placing a reverse downward pressure on the barrel and reducing powder gas pressures as they leave the muzzle.

How a shooter grips a shotgun can also help combat recoil. Taking a reasonably snug grip, along with stiffening one's wrists, will help absorb some recoil energy. Another recoil-reducing gun technique, known as "stretching the gun," was developed by the British. Upon trigger pull, the back hand applies rearward pressure while the front hand pushes aggressively forward. This push-pull action locks the gun between a shooter's hands as the recoil runs its course. This method calls for careful timing at the shot, which requires a little practice to master.

Thus waterfowlers don't have to endure the punishment meted out by heavy, magnum loads. By applying some of the aforementioned gun modifications and using a proper gun gripping technique, your shooting will be much more pleasant and productive the next time you visit the marsh or shooting range.

chapter forty-one

On Really Cleaning a Shotgun

When it comes to shotgun cleaning, the bore is often the main focus. Oh, a hunter may wipe the receiver and bolt with an oily rag, but it is the bore that gets most of the attention. If it shines like polished glass, many hunters are satisfied.

But although it's wise to take preventive measures against bore rusting and pitting, there's a lot more to cleaning a shotgun. The inner working parts should receive some TLC, too. Ask any seasoned gunsmith and he'll tell you that many shotgun problems are due to nothing more than a buildup of "gunk." This can be anything from bits of twigs and weed seeds to powder residue, carbon, or corrosion from condensation or an outright soaking in the rain. Such gunk can act as an abrasive to hasten part wear, or it can block the operating components and cause malfunctions. Indeed, many who blame a repeater's design and assembly for failures are often themselves at fault for not cleaning the gun thoroughly. The bore has nothing to do with mechanical cycling.

Many are the hunters who claim no skills in stripping a sporting arm, but that can be a cop-out. Most sporting arms are packed with an instruction booklet that details takedown procedures. The instructions are commonly classics in simplicity. Anyone who can legitimately obtain hunting and driving licenses should be able to follow them.

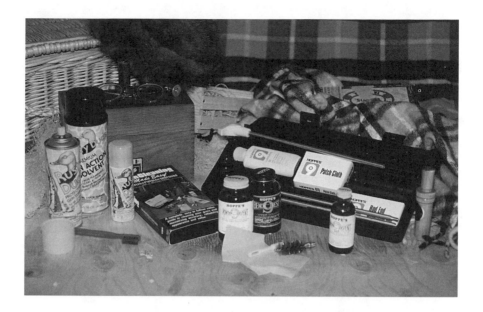

After each dunking, or at least at the end of the hunting season, follow the manufacturer's booklet and do a thorough job on the gun's action parts. Corrosion is more likely here than in the bore. The first takedown may be an adventure for those who aren't mechanically inclined, but after that initial foray into the unknown it will become easier. Whenever possible, remove the stock from the receiver and clean and dry this juncture. When this area of the stock is dry, apply some tung oil or Tru-Oil.

As a final point, always try to use hollow-ground screwdrivers that fit the slots to prevent mashing screw heads. I'm hardly a poet, but this couplet explains shotgun cleaning:

There's more
Than the bore!

See Clearly Now

During one of my first hunting seasons back in the 1940s, my father and I parked the '34 Plymouth on a gravel road and headed toward a spot along the river where mallards and woodies had been dropping in for a morning's dabble. We had to break through a dense cover in the darkness before dawn.

Powered by youthful enthusiasm, I was in high gear—until I impaled my right eye on a willow twig! Lights flashed and tears flowed! For several minutes I stood head down, my hand cupping a painful eye. After the immediate sting faded, I could barely open either eye's lids. Luckily, no permanent damage was done.

I am thus no hypocrite when I advocate glasses with enlarged lenses for safety afield. Not only do they shield one's eyes from twigs and the slap of branches, but they also reduce the impact of wind-driven debris.

And there's much more to the selection of hunting and shooting glasses than safety. The matters of fit and optimal vision are equally important. Indeed, hunters who buy discount store sunglasses are robbing themselves of optical efficiency, for there's a world of difference between plain ol' sunglasses and bona fide shooting/hunting eyewear.

Shooting glasses are a must in the duck blind or target field, protecting eyes from hazards and debris, and cutting down on reflection and glare.

One such difference pivots on lens geometry. Many sunglasses have flat lenses, whereas the human eye is known as a six-curve eye, and lenses should be ground to match that ophthalmic shape. Even curved lenses on over-the-counter sunglasses don't always provide the shape.

Moreover, each individual should be measured for precise fit and pupillary distance to place the focal centers perfectly. Mass-produced sunglasses simply can't match each hunter. The optical industry also tries for a 12mm eye-to-lens distance. If this distance isn't established, the power and clarity will be upset. Thus, to maintain eye-to-lens distance, the frames should have adjustable nose pads, brow bar, and temple pieces. And they should be professionally fitted.

Also, shooting glasses are made to ride higher than are basic sunglasses and reading glasses. This slight elevation lifts the frame above the line of vision as a hunter lowers his head to the comb and places the optical centers where the eyes look when a shooter's head is down.

chapter forty-two

What about color? There are two distinctly different considerations here. The clay shooter wants colors that will (1) produce target contrast and (2) provide optimal light transmission. The various oranges, browns, reds, and purples are used mainly to make orange targets stand out sharply under various light and background situations. Optimal light transmission is useful to allow the pupil to supply the brain with the sharpest picture and greatest depth of field.

Hunters needn't concern themselves with contrast, as there are few orange geese and ducks. Instead, hunters must think in terms of retained natural colors and ample light transmission. These are the varying shades of green and neutral gray, which are also easy on one's eyes during a daylong hunt.

When shopping for hunting or shooting glasses, be aware of the many coatings now available. These include anti-reflectance, blue-blocking, and ultraviolet coatings.

Also realize that glass is practically passé in sport glasses these days. Many modern plastics are now lighter and stronger than glass, so shop around before you buy. There are a lot of subtleties in modern, high-quality hunting and shooting eyewear.

Clothes Make the Man

There was a time when my home state's waterfowl season ran into freezing weather and early snows, and I enjoyed those days immeasurably. My college days of the 1950s were especially great, and from them I learned something about preparing for cold-weather wingshooting.

I commuted to college, and in the trunk of my relic 1941 Chevy were hunting clothes, decoys, loads, and my 20-gauge Remington Model 11-48 Sportsman. When I didn't have afternoon classes I took my heavy wear into the men's locker room of the gymnasium and changed to long johns and bulky woolens, the standard garb of the day. Then I funneled myself into a pair of chest-high waders and pointed the hood of the Chevy toward a farmland pothole where I could still stomp open the ice, or toward a spot along the river where fast water remained ice free. The shotgunning part of all this stems from some mysterious misses on such frigid days, when those big, twin-curl greenheads came swooshing in. The birds were right there, 20 to 25 yards out, and I missed them. Likewise, I whiffed on some crossing mallards at 30 to 40 yards. This was puzzling because I'd made those same shots back in October and early November.

I brooded about those misses while I sat in lecture halls, but the answer didn't come until one day when I rushed from a lab course to the car for my gear and a quick change. The heavy woolens weren't there. But I did have a pair of light longies in my zipper bag, and the waders were bunched in the backseat. Rather than miss one of the last days of the season, I went hunting in that light garb. And after I'd set the decoys in some slow water below a gentle rapids, I pushed back into the cover and began to shiver.

That was the day my shooting came back, and I finally unraveled the mystery of the cold-weather misses. One drake didn't quite trust the spread. After his fifth swing I got ready, and as he sped atop the trees on the far side of the river I swung the Remington past him, extended the forward allowance, and buckled him with a 1-ounce pattern of No. 5s. I was more than happy to stumble through the rapids to make my retrieve. It was then that I knew what had changed: It was the clothes.

Bulky wear is anathema to good shotgunning. It binds the shoulders, hinders the pivot, makes the gun fit differently. When I didn't wear my woolens, I was free to swing the gun as I had during the early season.

For hunters who expect to face extreme weather conditions, the points should be obvious: (1) don't overdress; (2) keep the layers as

©BILL BUCKLEY

This hunter in Denmark proves that what you wear afield can be influenced by more than weather conditions.

©CHUCK PETRIE

light, as supple, and as few as possible; and (3) always check out the fit of a shotgun relative to the build-up of clothing layers. One of the major mistakes made in gun buying is the failure to appreciate the impact that added shoulder bulk will have on a gun's stock dimensions. What feels perfect to you on a summer evening in a gun shop will suddenly become a poor, ineffective fit when you're hunkered in a big parka with insulation and a gun patch pushing the butt well away from your shoulder.

The most important part of good gunning in cold weather, then, is how well you can point and swing the fowling piece when you're dressed against the temperature. A concern for gun fit and pivot is essential. Regardless of the cold, modern shotshells still tend to give ballistics that are adequate for legitimate sporting ranges. But can you put the pattern where it belongs if you're dressed to look like the Michelin Man?

Have Shotgun, Will Travel, But...

Men may snicker about the way women fuss over which clothes they'll pack for a trip, but they'd better do the same when selecting a shotgun for foreign travel.

One consideration is gun fit and recoil. Remember that as a stateside hunter you fire but a few loads on each hunt. However it's not uncommon to experience more shooting opportunities when traveling to destinations where game bird concentrations are greater. This introduces the recoil factor.

On a South American dove hunt, I met a man whose fine Browning 12-gauge Superposed didn't fit him, and while firing a large number of shells on the first day, he developed a "mouse" under his eye. For the rest of his expensive trip, he had pain on every shot.

If you don't know whether your shotgun will bruise you during extended firing, take it to a skeet or trap field and get in at least a hundred shots. The practice will sharpen you for the trip, and if you feel abusive recoil, you can have the stock altered or you can pick a different gun. Knowledgeable travelers often leave their doubles at home and take gas-operated autoloaders for their softer recoil.

Always take a full set of choke tubes. You never know how changes in weather will affect shooting distances. To date, most other nations still permit lead shot for waterfowl, so take those chokes indicated for the type of pellet, be it steel or lead, that you intend to use.

chapter forty-four

Breakdowns can plague a trip. A pair of precautions can guard against this disaster: First, if possible, carry a pair of guns. Second, ask a gunsmith which part(s) of your gun is the most likely to falter, and carry a spare plus whatever tools are needed to change it. Don't expect to find a well-stocked gunsmith on the Argentine Pampas or in the Cauca Valley of Colombia! (An emergency repair kit for the Remington Models 1100 and 11-87 is available from Shooting Accessories Ltd. by calling toll-free 800-676-8920.) Also, be sure to carry some gun-cleaning equipment to ward off corrosion and to keep the guns ticking. This is especially important for waterfowling trips or hunts in hot, humid regions.

Finally, always make certain that you obtain complete information from your outfitter or travel agent regarding the customs procedures. Often paperwork, including the gun serial number, is required. That's why it's so important to give your gun selection serious thought during the planning stages, as gun permits must frequently be filed long before the trip. If in doubt, ask precise questions of your outfitter or the respective nation's stateside embassy.